"Get ready for teens to rule the world—*Stay Strong* gives them wisdom that could only come from a seasoned pro."
—*Russell Simmons,*
CEO 360HipHop and Rush Communications
Founder, Def Jam Records

"In this remarkable collection, Terrie Williams craftily weaves moral truths with practical instruction for today's youth. Inspired by her own journey in the entertainment industry, Williams lends teenagers a personal, triumphant model for success."
—*Montel Williams, author and host of* THE MONTEL WILLIAMS SHOW

"A modern affirmation of the power of possibility, *Stay Strong* provides you with hip advice on how to think and act outside the box."
—*Charlie Ward, NY Knicks point guard*

"*Stay Strong* exposes you to the power often locked within. This useful guide seeks to help you become the intelligent, imaginative, and innovative young thinkers you are destined to be."
—*Johnnie Cochran, attorney*

"There are several words to describe this book; practical, wise, heartening, *essential*. . . need I go on?"
—*Tavis Smiley, author and host of* BET Tonight

"As good a read as this book promises to be, reading it is not enough; you must use it early and often."
—*Chris Cuomo, ABC News magazine* 20/20, *correspondent*

STAY S

SCHOLASTIC INC.

New York Toronto London Auckland Sydney
Mexico City New Delhi Hong Kong Buenos Aires

TRONG

Simple Life Lessons for Teens

WITH AN INTRODUCTION BY QUEEN LATIFAH

BY TERRIE WILLIAMS

 • ISBN 0-439-12972-9 Published by Scholastic Inc. • 12 11 10 9 8 7 6 5 3 4 5 6/0 • Printed in the U.S.A. • First Scholastic paperback printing, October 2001 • Text type was set in Adobe Garamond • Book design by Elizabeth Parisi • Cover art © 2001 by McDavid Henderson

For Susan L. Taylor . . .

the promise and the friendship

TABLE OF CONTENTS

INTRO-DUCTION

It's a tough world out there.

I know . . . you're probably thinking: "What does Queen Latifah know about tough? She's a celebrity. She's a TV star. She's a rich and famous singer. She doesn't know anything about the *real world.*"

OK . . . it's true that I am now very, very blessed to be "making it." But I'm telling you — and this comes straight from the heart — I *do* know what goes on in the real world. I wasn't born in the recording studio, or running a business, or on the set of a popular television show. The CDs and the TV programs weren't just given to me. It took years and years of hard work and relentless dedication to get where I am today.

And trust me — I know what it's like to be young, to have to struggle with friends, family and schoolwork. I know what it's like to have problems — my parents got divorced when I was young so I'm familiar with the challenges a lot of you are facing. And, as some of you may know, my brother Lance was killed in a motorcycle accident, and I had to try and understand why someone so close to me had to die so young. I also know that we're all human and we make mistakes. There's a lot of temptation and a lot of peer presure, and sometimes it's hard to make the right decision.

But what I really, really know is that you, too, *can* make it. You can do whatever you want to do, be whatever you want to be, and be a success. *If* you work hard at everything you do, and if you really look inside yourself and decide that you want to be a good person.

That's what this book is about. Terrie Williams truly cares about other folks — especially young people like you. She's good people, and she wrote this book to try and help you to be a success — in life and in whatever you want to do. What she's not is just another adult trying to tell you what to do or talk down at you.

Don't look at it that way. Terrie's cool, and she knows what she's talking about. And, as you'll see as you read this book, she's talked to and hung out with a lot of kids who probably feel the same way you do about a lot of things.

I know what it's like to be a teenager — it wasn't *that* long ago that I was your age, and I remember having the funny feelings about growing up. You may think that you're different from other kids. Or that all the pressures of school, and trying to be popular and trying to fit in are gonna just build up and make you crazy. I've been there. I've done that. And like I said, you'll see throughout this book that there are a whole bunch of kids out there just like you.

But what I'm saying — and what Terrie says in this book — is don't worry about it too much. You can get through all this stuff. Your teachers can help. Your parents can help. (My parents were a big influence on me when I was growing up. My mom is a teacher — one of the greatest jobs in the world — and she's always talking to and helping her kids. And my dad was a police officer who was always helping others.) Even your friends can help. And — believe it or not — you can help your friends. We should all be here for each other.

Sure you're always going to come across someone who's different, or who might seem a bit strange. Maybe other folks think *you're* a bit different. But it's OK to be special in your own way — in your style, your choice of music, the things you want to do, and the way you want to be. We're all different. I mean, how many other Queen Latifahs do you know?

Most important, though, we're also all the same. We're all just human beings trying to make it. You'll find that out by reading *Stay Strong.*

It's a tough world out there.

But if you remain true to who you are and take these life lessons to heart, you'll find that things can be a little easier. Maybe it won't happen overnight. Maybe you'll have to work pretty hard at trying to change some things in your life. And maybe you'll make some mistakes. But if you learn from those mistakes, and if you really try to be cool to everyone you meet, and be a righteous person — I guarantee you good things will happen.

And maybe the world won't be such a tough place. Take it from Queen Latifah.

Peace.

BEFORE YOU START, READ THIS...

My name is Terrie Williams, and I've written this book to help make you — and everyone around you — feel better. I've got my own business that handles publicity for entertainers, athletes, and big corporations. That means I work with those celebrities or companies to get good stories about them in newspapers and magazines and on TV shows and radio programs. When I opened my agency in 1988, Eddie Murphy was the first person to sign up. Through the years I've worked with such recording artists as Janet Jackson, Boyz II Men, Master P, and Sean "Puffy" Combs; high-profile lawyer Johnnie

Cochran; best-selling thriller author Stephen King; talk-show host Sally Jessy Raphael; and sports heroes like Jackie Joyner-Kersee and NBA players Jerry Stackhouse and Charlie Ward, as well as NBA and NFL teams.

Often I accept engagements to participate in conferences as a speaker or panelist. Others find it helpful and encouraging to hear about my experiences. I share them because it is important to me to help others and if I have some information that will benefit people in their life or business, I want them to know it. Mostly I do it as a way of repaying those who have shared their insights with me — and those who help keep me going with their wisdom and advice. It's how we keep the cycle going. It's an amazing feeling.

Young people have always held a very special place in my heart. I've talked, mentored, and listened to hundreds of you over the years. I believe I've learned a lot from you about what it's like to be a teenager today. And because you have taught me in many ways how to laugh and have fun, I wanted to give you something back — hence, this book.

I have been pretty successful, and kids often ask me how I accomplished it. What did I do to get paid to hang with celebrities and actually do work that helps people? Was I supersmart, special? Did my parents have pull? Was I super "fine" or hot? Did I just have a lot of breaks?

The answer to all these questions is no. Now, I was pretty smart. I've been told I'm not bad to look at, and I've had my share of blessings and plain old luck. But, I went through the same stuff as you . . . and still do.

In this book I'm sharing some of things I have found to be important in getting what you want out of life. You get what you want out of life by being different from everyone else. Not different in a bad way; different in a cool way — a way that will earn you props from your friends, your teachers, your family, and everybody you deal with. In my first book, I called this unique way of life "The Personal Touch." I'm glad to say it's helped a lot of people in their business and personal lives. Over time, a lot of clients have become more than just business associates, and I'm proud to even call some of them friends. I've shared with them my Personal Touch secrets and ideas, and they love 'em! They hear what I'm saying and they find my advice very helpful.

For you, as teens, the Personal Touch begins by

turning around the way most people think about life and having a different attitude. That attitude says that one person — you — can be different and *make* a difference. It says that the little things — the things *you* can do — matter. It says that you don't have to see results of doing good right now, but that you have to trust that what goes around comes around.

So, each chapter of this book takes an attitude that is accepted in today's world and shows you how that attitude is wrong. I help you adopt a new attitude that will make you feel great about yourself and put you on the road to getting what you really want from life.

I promise you: This stuff works. Yes, it's going to break some rules. I'm going to ask you to look at attitudes that "everybody" has — on fairness (no, life isn't fair, but can *you* be?); lying (isn't *somebody* in your life a truth-teller?); getting and having money (is it really all about the Benjamins?); talking and not talking; manners and how to treat people; time; feelings and lots more.

I'm going to challenge you to make up your mind to have a different attitude than "everybody" else has. I'll give you examples of how to work these new attitudes into your life that won't always be easy, but *will* make you — and everyone around you — feel better. And as you grow up, these attitudes and actions *will* get you what you really want out of life.

In this book I'll help you understand that what you think and feel isn't all that different from what anybody else is going through. I'll also help you handle your everyday problems so that you deal better with stressful situations and with other people. I want to introduce you to choices you can make *now* that will make a difference in your life.

You'll see quotes and stories from teenagers throughout the book. I wanted to give you the thoughts, feelings, ideas, and situations of other teens, so some friends and I interviewed dozens of young people. Their words are sprinkled into mine. Some kids are from high school, some are from after-school programs. They're probably a lot like you. Their names have been changed to protect the innocent *and* the guilty! They let you know that you're not alone. They know what it's like to be growing up, to feel the pressure to do well. They speak from their experience with school, grades, family, sex, drugs, the peer demands to do things you may not want to do. They, like you, are forming their personal values.

They may think or feel the same way you do. I hope their words will make you think seriously about your own attitudes.

As I share a little of what I've learned in life, in business with lots of celebs, and from teens, I hope that you start to dream big dreams for your life and that you start to achieve them now. Stay strong and in the race.

Terrie Williams

New York, June 2000

"We are reading about the Crusades in school. That surely wasn't fair. I can't do nothing about things like that."
— Joshua

"So what can you do?" — Kevin

Okay. Life ain't fair, but what you do does matter. A young man was shot at an after-school basketball program at a high school in Brooklyn. Star basketball player and point guard for the New York Knicks Charlie Ward went to share some words of support with the kids in the program, just because he was touched by the unfair hand life had dealt them. What do you do when you see an unfair situation?

Reggie Harris, who was a beloved and respected news reporter in New York for twenty years, died suddenly. Charlie Ward had met Reggie and his son once and wanted to send a card to the family. I remembered that Reggie's son was a huge basketball fan, so I suggested that Charlie invite him to a basketball game. Charlie gave Darren Harris and his friend two tickets to a Knicks game — and believe me those tickets are hard to get! I picked up the boys and took them to the family room, to the prayer service that the Knicks have before every game, and to the locker room after the game. Darren's thank-you note afterward said it was the most fun he'd had since his father had died. These are the types of things that make life worth living even when we see unfair things happening to people all around us.

Maybe you can't do as much as you'd like to do, but you can do something. A thirteen-year-old boy was dying of leukemia at New York's Memorial Sloan-Kettering Hospital. One of his last wishes was to meet Eddie Murphy. But Eddie's film schedule wouldn't allow him to get to New York City. So, we bought a tape recorder and had Eddie record a message for the boy. Eddie gave him one of his personally monogrammed bathrobes, a poster, and a photograph signed to him. The boy was disappointed that he couldn't meet Eddie personally — but he did leave this world with a smile on his face. His mother said it was the greatest gift he could have had. He listened to the tape repeatedly and slept with the tape recorder under his pillow.

A major fire spread throughout Malibu, California, and several homes were destroyed. It took a good deal of time and energy to fight the fire. Of her own accord, Janet Jackson decided to provide massage therapists to the entire fire department. Maybe you can't fight the fire, but you can do something. Think about what Janet did. Being creative in an unfair situation means a lot.

It is not fair that there are children in the world who don't get to have a childhood because they are working for low wages for their own survival or to help their families. Is it fair that children are basically used as slave labor to chop sugarcane on plantations in Brazil or to work in clothing sweatshops in Asia? Of course not.

Well, Craig Kielburger from Canada, who is sixteen years old, decided it wasn't fair, either — so he started a foundation called Free the Children, dedicated to eliminating child labor. I read about him in *People* magazine and *The New York Times.* As a result of his efforts, many young people have gotten involved in helping to make the world a better place. Under Craig's leadership, Free the Children has influenced popular manufacturers, like Nike and Guess, to not use child labor in their factories abroad. The foundation has even influenced the government of Brazil to spend money to get children to go to school rather than the sugarcane plantations. You see, life isn't fair, but what you do does matter. Three things you can do when you face unfair situations are:

TAKE THE HIGH ROAD

Taking the high road means doing the difficult thing because it is right. Most people want to do the quickest, easiest thing. The right thing requires more of us.

In *Newsday,* a New York daily newspaper, an article called "Balancing Act" was all about a girl named Daisy Sanchez. Daisy was very active in sports, but the story reported that she was going to have to give up a lot of her sports activities in order to help her mother support their family:

"But family ties cannot obscure the fact that caring for [her brother and sister] will keep Daisy tied to home for the next two seasons. What she *wants* to do is join the rifle team in the winter and play softball in the spring. What she *has* to do is go straight to a job when classes are over in order to help support her family, then go home to take care of Cynthia, nine, and Brandon, three.

"Her mother, Rosa, works twelve-hour days at a commercial laundry to support her family, then goes to night school to learn English and take a computer class. Daisy's mother might be pulling her away from sports, but Daisy refuses to blame Rosa.

"'I don't think it's her fault,' Daisy says . . . 'we just have to stick by each other and help each other out.'"

This young woman could be bitter or angry because she is not going to get to do what she wants to do. But by helping out her family and not blaming her mother, she has taken the high road.

In *Chicken Soup for the Teenage Soul,* there is a story of a girl who dropped her friends from kindergarten for new friends when she got older. Her old friends invited her to their birthday parties and bat mitzvahs and bar mitzvahs (Jewish rights of passage into adulthood), but she did not reciprocate when her parties came up. She invited her new friends. Somewhere along the way she was excluded from the new group, though. Slowly she worked her way back into her old group. They accepted her from the start. They would have been well within their rights to avoid her. They took the high road. Their attitude was to understand rather than condemn and exclude.

Taking the high road may just be an attitude or a response to a certain situation. My company is a full-service public relations, marketing, and communications firm. We work with people in different industries, from entertainment to politics. Some of the people I represent today dissed me at one time or another. It used to make me angry; then I realized I'd take it as a vitamin. It fortified me.

I worked with a well-known producer and director on an organization he founded to assist filmmakers and directors. After about a year with the organization he decided he wanted his friend to take over, leaving me out. I oriented the new person to her job and moved on. I had found their first office and helped set things up. I was the first program administrator, and because I had put so much development into the organization I wanted to remain involved on the board. The producer/director told me I couldn't be on the board because I wasn't a big enough name, that the organization had stars on the board and only wanted famous names there. To this day I have been very helpful to the founder of the organization. Many years later the producer/director and I reconnected and I was honored by the organization for my contributions. Take the high road. The high road always winds its way back to something good.

KNOW THAT WHAT GOES AROUND COMES AROUND

You're gonna hear me say this a million times because I believe it is a universal principle.

A teenager like you said, "If you treat life as though nothing is fair, then you will experience nothing good." You can treat people in a mean way, but it will come back to you. It could be in an obvious way: Your friends could reject you. Or it could be more subtle. The principal could have observed your behavior and changed his or her mind about recommending you for a job. You just never know. Because "what goes around comes around," life can be fairer than we know. And this goes for positive actions as well as negative ones. You may gain a lot of personal satisfaction because you've done something good for a friend, family member, or even a stranger — and that kind of act could result in an unexpected honor.

A couple had been married for about twenty-five

years, had ten children, and had never been on a vacation. Eddie Murphy read about them and decided on his own to treat them to a vacation with five thousand dollars in spending money. Once word got out about that, Merv Griffin, who owns several resorts, ended up paying for the couple's hotel stay. Their kindness helped the family — and it probably helped their careers, too. When people find out nice things about celebrities, people perceive them differently. A generous gesture might open new doors for them — more people will admire them for new reasons, and more people will want to work with them, too.

When Charlie Ward visited the school where the young basketball player was killed, it wasn't for the sake of getting attention. He went to talk to the kids because he cared. His visit was mentioned in a follow-up article to the story. A sports columnist from *The New York Times* happened to see the item, was very impressed, and decided to do a huge article on Charlie. In the end, his caring gesture was noticed by the Knicks management, the NBA, and the readership of the *Times.* He came out looking really good.

Just knowing you've done a good thing can be reward enough. But when you do good, it's like reaping and sowing. Walk the earth righteously. Everything that goes around comes around. Honestly, that's what keeps me from being evil sometimes. What keeps me going in a challenging situation is that I know it's coming back. It is the law of nature.

GIVE THE BENEFIT OF THE DOUBT

It's unfair from where you stand, but you may not have the whole story.

REAL STORIES

Claire, Natasha, and Mr. Sommers's Art Class

Claire had been in Mr. Sommers's art class all year. Some of her work had been good. He had given her an A on her romance-book cover project. She got a C on the children's book. (The story was better than the artwork.) She got a B+ on the collage project. It took a little longer to grasp the idea of the collage — by the time she realized it could be anything, she didn't have enough time to imagine something spectacular. Still, though Claire had to work on her figure drawing, she was a better than average student, with a solid B average in art class.

Natasha sat across from Claire in class. She had come into Mr. Sommers's class late in the year. Her family had come to America from eastern Europe. She spoke little English. For the most part she did exceptional work. But family problems caused Natasha to miss at least one day of school during the week — and often, that day was the same day as art class.

For their final project, the class had to take an article from the newspaper or a report from the television news and create a piece that used techniques and mediums they had studied during the year. Claire got a B- on her project, but it didn't affect her average that much: She was still a solid B student. Natasha, however, finished with an A+ average.

Claire was beside herself. How could that be? Sure, the girl was a good artist. But she was hardly ever there. Since she was absent, she had gotten the assignment a week later than everyone else. It wasn't fair.

Every one of Claire's friends agreed that Mr. Sommers was being unfair. In fact, Malik was ready to get a petition together for everyone to sign. But Claire wanted to handle it on her own. She went to Mr. Sommers.

"I don't think it's fair that you gave Natasha an A+ for this class. She was out more than she was here," Claire said.

"Natasha is a very good artist, Claire," he replied.

"But she just got her assignment. Some of us worked really hard in this class. You said back in September that attendance was a part of the grade. Some of us were here every week. That should count for something."

"I think Natasha deserves an A+ and that's what I gave her. What's done is done."

Claire wanted to say, "I think you should change her grade right now!" But instead she felt defeated.

Mr. Sommers continued, "What do you want me to do?"

"Nothing," she replied. "I just wanted to say, I don't think it's fair."

She picked up her portfolio and walked out of class.

The between-class rush swirled around her. Kids shouted to one another — where they were going to meet, what class was next, who just got a job. She heard the slamming of lockers and the shriek of girls who got dates with cool guys.

She walked past the cafeteria. Suddenly, she turned back and shoved her portfolio into the huge garbage can by the door. Then a couple of jocks tossed in the remains of their spaghetti-and-meatball lunch. Claire pushed through the doors out to the commons, barely keeping back the tears. She sat on a bench for a while, feeling sorry for herself. Then she went back to the trash can and pulled out her portfolio with two fingers. She scraped it along the edge of the garbage can and went into the cafeteria to get some napkins.

Some kids get A's and B's and hardly ever have to study, while you have to bust your butt to keep your grade point average up. But the time and energy you put in will pay off in more than just good grades. You will have gained study skills, self-discipline, and perhaps even some knowledge that will benefit you later in life.

Claire could take comfort in the fact that she spoke up and was strong enough to go to Mr. Sommers even if it didn't change anything. She had the ability to voice what she thought was right. She could have gathered a group of angry students around her, yet she chose to go on her own. She thought about giving up and decided not to.

It's not enough to go in and whine because the teacher gave one person an A and you a B. In a courteous manner, ask why this has happened. Look your teacher in the eye. Have an open mind and be ready to listen. Think ahead to the next thing you want to say. You may learn something you didn't know.

The fact is that there may have been circumstances Claire didn't know about. For example, maybe the school or Mr. Sommers had an agreement with Natasha and her family. Maybe they decided to keep quiet as long as Natasha's work was done.

We don't see everything. We don't know everything. Sometimes you have to give a person or situation the benefit of the doubt. It may not be fair, but it doesn't have to bum you out.

In the long run, Claire chose to cope with the situation even though she didn't like it. She could consider it a challenge to do better the next time around.

So, when life seems unfair, take the high road, know that what goes around comes around, and give people the benefit of the doubt. And, then look for examples to inspire you to create fairness.

Hydeia L. Broadbent, a fifteen-year-old girl, is an example of rising above life's injustices. Her mother abandoned Hydeia (pronounced hy-day-ah) when she was born. Hydeia was born with HIV from her mother's drug use and has been living with full-blown AIDS since the age of five. Hydeia had no choice about her health when she was born. It's not fair. But having HIV has not stopped Hydeia from living a full life. She enjoys riding her bike, dancing, and ice skating. Not only does she enjoy her leisure activities, she has become an activist.

According to *Essence* magazine, Hydeia "has become a most eloquent spokesperson for those in her generation with AIDS. She lectures regularly to schools and universities around the country, has appeared on television talk shows, and spoke at the Republican National Convention in 1996 . . . In every instance she brings a message of hope, encouragement, and love to those afflicted with this terrible disease, while educating those who misunderstand it."

It is unfair for a child to be born with AIDS. Her

adoptive parents, Patricia and Lorin Broadbent, have given Hydeia tremendous support — and it doesn't end there. When Hydeia was seven or eight she convinced her family to take in another child with HIV.

As far as I am concerned, Hydeia is an angel. She received an *Essence* Award in 1999. Her life and her example are an inspiration. Comedian Chris Rock also received an *Essence* Award that year. He was so moved and impressed with Hydeia and the Broadbent family that he gave his award to Hydeia's mother. He announced that he personally did not deserve the award, then he walked down from the stage and into the audience to put his award in Patricia Broadbent's hand.

With the help of her family, Hydeia has overcome the unfair circumstances of her life. She is leading with strength and courage.

Amber Coffman is also a powerful person.

She is eighteen years old and lives in Glen Burnie, a suburb of Baltimore, Maryland. She was crowned Miss Teen Maryland in 1997, when she was only fifteen. Sure, she's attractive on the outside, but her true beauty comes from within. When she was ten years old, she did a class project on Mother Teresa and, inspired by her example, decided to reach out to the poor in the Baltimore area. So seven years ago, Amber founded the nonprofit corporation Happy Helpers for the Homeless and became its CEO (chief executive officer). With the help of her mother, Bobbi, some friends, and some local merchants, Amber and her team assemble and take some seven hundred sandwiches and pastries to the poor in downtown Baltimore every week.

Amber and her mom have had their own disappointments and difficulties. She did not place among the ten finalists in the Miss Teen USA pageant. More hurtful, though, was the time one of the homeless people threw a cup of ice in her face when there was no more Kool-Aid. Not fair, right? The article from *The Washington Post Magazine* records her response: "'I couldn't believe it.' Amber recalls. 'It was like, here we are trying to do something nice for him and he throws it back in our face. But I guess when you're thirsty you don't really think about your reactions.'"

Another inspiring teenager is eighteen-year-old Robert Johnson. I first heard his story on *Oprah.* When he was ten years old he got caught in the crossfire of rival gangs and was blinded. Now Robert reads Braille, plays the piano, and studies sound engineering in college. His response to what happened to him is,

"If this hadn't happened, I probably would have gotten involved or trapped in drugs and illegal things."

Many Grammy-, Emmy-, and Oscar-winning songs, movies, and performances come out of the tragedies of ordinary people. You must count your blessings no matter how they disguise themselves.

REACHING OUT

Life isn't fair. That's real. But you're not alone. You have your family and your friends to take you through the rough times. Do your part to create fairness because what you do *does* matter.

Reach out to people you know are outsiders. Be a friend to them. Bring them into your group. If you're on the outside and feel like an outcast, reach back when someone extends a friendly hand. Are you one of those students who doesn't have to study very hard to get an A? Offer to tutor someone.

You can mentor a young person. When I speak and write about mentoring to business professionals I talk about establishing relationships. There are many ways you can *be* a mentor. Maybe you can help by tutoring. Maybe there's a kid at your place of worship who'd enjoy hanging out with an older kid who cares. You will reap untold benefits and so will the person to whom you have given your time. Here's an example from my own life.

I was once out of town with a client and had scheduled a hectic, filled-to-the-brim day of meetings. A former intern (now a reporter), Jocelyn Coleman had kept in touch and knew I'd be visiting this city, where two of her friends were starting their own public relations business. Would I mind meeting them briefly? Jocelyn asked. Of course not, I said, and we set up a time in the evening to meet at my hotel. The day's events took much, much longer than I had expected, and I didn't get back to the hotel until almost midnight. The two young entrepreneurs, however, had waited for me. Even though I was dragging, I knew I could not turn them away. So we went to my room, where we chatted until well after one in the morning. And as tired as I was, I still felt good after our meeting. Passing it on always puts a smile on my face. The only thing I ask of people when I help them is to do something for someone else.

When you take time to help someone — and it doesn't have to be a lot — you can have a positive effect on another life. That person will remember you as someone who made them feel special and that will come in handy when they are either feeling down or have the opportunity to pass it on to another person.

GIVING BACK

Nieves Diaz, a seventeen-year-old high school senior, was named 1999 Youth Volunteer of the Year by the Cross Island, New York, YMCA. She is making a difference right in her own backyard. She got involved in giving back because, she said, "When I was younger, I wished there were people around to help me. So I made a decision to do it . . ." Among her activities, she is the youth member of the YMCA's program/membership committee, teen center, and after-school child-care program. She also organized a Leaders Club community service project at the Bowery Street Mission in Lower Manhattan. Her reason to volunteer, as she told New York *Newsday:* "It makes you feel good and you get to enjoy it. Everyone thinks there are other people out there who will do things. But if you don't do it, who will?"

Monica Vaughn-Cooke wanted to make a difference in children's lives. So she helped build a school for young students in Ghana. Cooke says her experience in the West African country was one she will never forget — so much so that it has influenced her decision to major in biomedical engineering this fall. "When I was in Ghana, I saw people who couldn't afford adequate health care," she says. "It made me see how much we take for granted here in the United States, and I wanted to improve health-care technology and make it affordable for them." As a result of her hard work and effort, Cooke was awarded a Prudential Spirit of Community Award, which recognizes young people for outstanding community service. Says Cooke: "I feel good, like I have accomplished something."

After a brutal beating by a carload of white kids, Jean-Dominque (JoJo) Catchings, who is black, decided to direct his rage into action. "My anger turned to concern," says Catchings, age nineteen. He started Speak Out Hot Line, a nonprofit twenty-four-hour hot line for teens in central Florida. The hot line has no recorders or caller ID and allows teens and their parents to call in anonymously. As a result of the hot line dozens of guns have been reported on school campuses. Young people have reported drug use, gang activity, and a computer whiz kid who produced fake IDs.

JoJo and his mother, Cheryl Catchings, speak at churches, schools, conferences, and community events. They are accompanied by a four-man singing group called Chivalry in which JoJo also sings. They encourage young people to live "clean lives — of sexual abstinence and nonviolence." JoJo's mom, who is also the director of the hot line, says, "Young people do want to participate in safety [programs] if we give them a chance. When I speak, I tell them that there is no such thing as a snitch when someone's life is in jeopardy. You are your brother's keeper and you must do your part to make sure the village is safe."

There was a real need for the hot line, which has been so successful that it has spread from JoJo's home county of Brevard in Florida to seven nearby counties.

As a result of his work, JoJo has received recognition by being awarded the Jacqueline Kennedy Onassis Award for outstanding public service.

You can make a difference! Stuff happens. Life's not fair. It's messed up. But we can decide how we are going to deal with it, because we know, one way or another, we *have* to deal with it. Even when we ignore the bad stuff, it still happens. It doesn't go away. We have to take action.

Life Ain't Fair Rap

what would you do if you had a choice / what would you do if you had a voice / to speak on the things you run into in life / that happen / and make you cry / that happen / and make you shout / that happen and make you call out / for justice and equality / for rightness and equanimity / for help when your life is more than you can bear / for help when you want somebody to care / put their arms around you and smother the fear and the fiery darts that sear / that burn and fuel your anger / put a hole in your heart / and make you start / to scream / it's not fair / you cry / it's not fair / you pull your hair / it's not fair! /

from jump street / someone shoulda tolja / you / were gonna have to be a soldier / life ain't fair / and won't be/

so don't be /

expecting it to be /

BUT / now / you know / and it's up to you how to respond / you don't need a golden eye like James Bond / just for your common sense to commence / decide you will not let this life beat you / eat you /

defeat you / upset you and let you drift away into oblivion / where you can't gain no dominion over the enemies of your life / you decide that / you choose that / you unloose the will in you to succeed / you supercede the pollution in the air that says, "Lie down, sucker, life ain't fair" / you decide that / you choose that / you unloose the will in you to succeed / to supercede / you supercede / you continue to dream / you no longer scream / puttin' your trust in God / don't let nobody make you feel odd / 'cause you put your trust in a higher power / or whatever/ you're not afraid from hour to hour / you don't despair / you don't pull out your hair / your life's on the go / you get on with the show / and it's old news to you 'cause you already know /that / life/ ain't / fair

— Sharita Hunt

"No one is fair. I just have to learn to live with unfairness and not let it bring me down." — Mary

"If I can make a difference, so can other kids." — Hannah

"Parents must teach kids about fairness and that what you do does matter." — Amy

"One person has the power to make a change in how things are. We just have to seize the moment." — Sonia

"If you see someone else flourishing in a field of work even if you think they got there unfairly, learn what you can from them." — Jennifer

"I know how it is to get dissed. So I just try to treat everyone with kindness." — Tatyana

"Stuff happens that you don't have control over; that's no excuse to be mean." — Chris

"My parents did a good job helping me to know how to treat people, no matter who they are." — Brandi

IT'S THE LITTLE THINGS

Think back to when you were a little kid. Think back to when you had a spectacular time with your mom and dad, grandmother or grandfather, aunt or uncle, or special adult in your life. Remember those moments that stand out in your mind, when you felt closest to the people you love. One of my friends has a Christmastime moment: making Christmas decorations with her mother. Another special moment was walking to the grocery story with her father, learning that it's proper for the man to walk on the outside. I would bet the things you remember are not necessarily the big trip to Disney World or all the presents you got during the holidays. More likely, it's the hands-on times with your family or friends when you connected, you had a sense of belonging, of being loved. It's the little things.

Life is about relationships. Even though it isn't fair, we've seen some things we can do to have a fulfilling life anyway.

- **Treat people the way you want to be treated.**
- **Let people know you appreciate them.**
- **Express gratitude.**

- Remember your manners.
- Ask for help – with school, when there's conflict – violence is not the answer!
- Study; stay in school.
- Stay real and be willing to cut others some slack – everybody has got some form of baggage or is hiding behind a mask.
- Tell the truth.
- Be kind to yourself and to others, eat healthy food, and get plenty of rest.
- Be about speaking with love and respect.
- Save and share your money – it's a tool.
- Give of your time and talents to your community.
- Talk – to your mom, your dad, a friend, a counselor, someone you trust when your thoughts or emotions seem all out of balance. Keeping it all inside is a slow poison.
- Go for it. Nothing beats a trial but a failure. (And we don't just get through failures, we grow through them.)
- Pay attention to your inner voice.
- Sometimes you just have to deal with things.
- Don't be so cool that you freeze people out.

Don't be afraid to change and always be willing to improve. In the book *Every Woman Has a Story* there's a quote, "We cannot become what we need to be by remaining what we are." When I read that, I highlighted it, knowing I had to share it with you. Be willing to change, and all the little things you do will add up to a significant and successful life. You may never become famous or fabulously rich but you will be someone who touches the lives of the people you meet in a meaningful way.

"Sure I lie. So what?" — Jennifer

"What's the big deal about telling a lie?" — Darron

"Some people lie to make friends. Some people lie to keep friends." — Regina

The reality is that people lie all the time. Here's one of my favorite stories about lying: I once hosted a reception for a very prominent celebrity. I had gotten one of my clients to pay for the reception. The celebrity and I were acquainted, but this celebrity went onstage and talked about how I was one of her very best friends! I was stunned because I couldn't believe she was going on and on without one iota of truth to her words.

Honesty is an important part of both your public life and your private life.

HONESTY IN YOUR COMMUNITY

Picture yourself in this situation:

REAL STORIES

James and Company or Finders' Keepers

James got off the bus. It was windy and cold for June. He finished his shift at Burger and Fries. He got his paycheck for working twenty hours at minimum wage. After taxes, his take-home pay was pitiful. As he headed toward home, he looked down and saw an envelope. For some reason, he picked it up. Inside was a grocery list and fifty dollars in cash.

Ah, man, he thought as he counted the money again.

Suddenly, it was the bad angel – good angel on-the-shoulder scene. The bad angel sounded suspiciously like Uncle Cecil, his mother's brother. "Shove the money in your pocket and keep going. Your girlfriend's birthday is next week and the day after tomorrow is Father's Day. With this money and your take-home pay you can get them both something nice and still have a little left over to put in the bank (which would make your mother very happy)."

The good angel sounded like his mother. "What if there are some poor hungry kids waiting for their father to return with milk and food?"

Then the bad angel said, "If the kids are starving, there should be food stamps in that envelope, sucker! This is cash, my man. Take it and keep steppin'."

"The least you can do is try to find the owner," the good angel said.

The bad angel intruded. "Excuse me. But there are eight million people in this city. And hundreds of thousands of people in this neighborhood alone. Hello."

Then the good angel said, "You have a grocery list. Whoever lost this money is going food shopping. Go to the store. See if anyone seems to have lost anything. If not, at least you tried." This bit of logic left the bad angel speechless.

So James walked toward the Shopwell supermarket near his building. He looked in front of the store and inside. He thought, *If I don't see a likely person, I'll take that as a sign to keep the money.* But no sooner had he thought this then he spotted a lanky kid in baggy pants patting himself, digging in his pockets, and looking around on the floor.

The bad angel said, "That's not him. Look at those pockets. You could lose four budget meals, the fry cook, and three customers in those pants. Whatever he lost, believe me, it's there. It's probably in his back pocket — down around his ankles."

The good angel said, "Then there's nothing to lose if you just ask him about the list."

The bad angel rolled his eyes. "Listen, you'd be doing the kid a favor. What better way to learn responsibility? He'll just have to face his mother. In the long run, you will have helped him with one more step to becoming a man."

James walked up to kid. "Are you looking for this?" he said, presenting the list.

The kid said, "Ah, man, yes! There was fifty bucks in an envelope, too. Ah, man."

James reached in his pocket and gave Baggy Pants the envelope.

As James left the store he figured he'd get his dad a polyester "silk" tie and his girlfriend a CD. At least he could afford that much.

He could have used the extra money, but he was cool. Baggy Pants was a kid like himself. He knew how it was to try and explain to your mom how you lost your lunch money. And fifty bucks was no joke. James was satisfied that he had done the right thing.

The bad angel said, "And what good did it do you? He didn't even say thank you. Chump!" The bad angel was so disgusted, he was gone as quickly as he'd come.

The good angel just smiled, hung around, and watched James, who seemed slightly taller, cross the street and head uptown to his building.

If James had found the fifty dollars in an envelope without the list or any clues about the owner, he might have kept it in good conscience. The bad angel had a good point. In a big city, any given neighborhood is like a small town. Any one of thousands of people could have lost the money. But James had a clue and his conscience would not let him ignore it. So he used his common sense and good judgment to try to find the person who had lost the money. James thought it was the right thing to do. It may sound corny, but you could say, "If I lost fifty bucks on the street, I would want someone to do the same thing for me."

We always have to choose whether we are going to behave or respond truthfully or falsely. The choices are often not easy. But if we pay attention, our conscience, the sense of right and wrong, is always there to guide us.

Be honest. I encourage you to do the right thing even when it involves hard decisions. Eventually you'll have to take responsibility for your own actions, so they might as well be good ones — or as good as you can make them.

Be honest with others regardless of who notices. You could be building a reputation that you don't even know about.

When you do the right thing, it makes you feel really good inside. (And you want to do it again.) It gives you strength. Believe me, integrity is a character trait you want to have. Even when there's conflict —

like Baggy Pants not saying thank you — you can take pride in doing what's right. You will not always be given gratitude or recognition — although they certainly feel good when you get them. But choosing the truthful way has a lasting effect that's empowering and will influence you the next time you have to make a choice. Make your choices based on who you are and what matters to you.

BE HONEST WITH / TO YOURSELF

Camryn Manheim, the Emmy Award-winning actress from the popular television show *The Practice,* has included a quiz in her book, *Wake Up, I'm Fat!* to give you clues about whether or not you love yourself. One of the questions is, "Do you tell yourself the truth?" So I ask, do you say, "I am an honest person," and then tell a lie? Do you tell yourself, "I'm a good person," yet talk about your friends when their backs are turned? What about, "I'm a good worker," but you goof off on the job?

When you get a B can you honestly say you did your best?

Are you honest with yourself about your looks, your intellect, and your relationships with family and friends? Do you look in the mirror and say to yourself, "Not bad"?

Keep honesty as a core value, not only when you're dealing with those around you but also when you're dealing with yourself. Let others know you're always learning. (Share what you learn with others.) Be willing to be honest about your gifts, talents, and interests. I believe that if you do, you'll have a lot more peace in your life — with fewer regrets.

Be honest with yourself. It can be hard, but check this out — you have gut responses and gut instincts and I encourage you to really listen to them.

Boom, boom, boom, boom, boom, boom, boom what's that beating / in your heart / in the part / where you desire, long for, aspire / is that a dream on the shelf? / Don't you conspire, burn up in fire, make you a liar, and let you go / you better use it before you lose it, before you lose that it belongs to you / people will laugh, try to break you in half, but you look in the mirror, and it gets clearer / that you have to live with you / look yourself in the eye and not flinch, it's a cinch you will wither let your dreaming self slither away / and exchange it / and change it / and arrange it so you fit in / so you sit in, and are welcome every bit in a place that you hate, and despise it / it burdens your eyes to see where you are / and it ain't the star that you thought / you bought less than you could, and more than you should and you didn't say whose is it anyway?/ whose is it anyway?/ whose is it anyway?

— Sharita Hunt

THE PRICE YOU PAY WHEN YOU LIE

Rob Pilatus and Fabrice Morvan were handsome and buff young men. They loved to dance and they wanted to be in show business. Then their dream came true. They had four hit songs that went to the top of the charts. They sold millions of singles and albums. They were awarded a Grammy in January 1990 for Best New Artist. Milli Vanilli was HOT!

They were on tour performing one night when something happened with the sound. The tape of the vocal arrangements broke. Milli Vanilli could not continue singing because, in fact, it was not their voices on the tape. The vocal sounds everyone had been grooving to were actually studio singers Brad Howell and John Davis. Pilatus and Morvan had only lip-synched. They'd faked it.

Other singers have used tape to help their singing when there is a lot of dancing, but they've always taped their own voices. In the case of Milli Vanilli, others were doing the singing and receiving neither public recognition nor profit.

Later it was reported that Milli Vanilli wanted to do their own singing, but since they weren't talented, their manager/producer refused. They fired him; he exposed them, and for the first time in Grammy history, the award was withdrawn. It was humiliating.

How did they get into such a mess? *Time* says, "They were living a marginal life in a Munich housing project when, in 1988, Farian [the producer] offered each of them $4,000 (plus subsequent royalties) to be seen but not heard as Milli Vanilli." They agreed.

After the scandal, they tried a comeback, but they never regained their reputation.

VH1's *Behind the Music* did a biography on the rise and fall of Milli Vanilli. We saw what their success brought them — the money and the fame. But we also saw that they were ultimately unable to deal with their instant success or their deception.

In 1998, Rob Pilatus died at the age of thirty-two of an apparent drug/alcohol overdose in Frankfurt, Germany. *E! OnLine News* quoted former Milli Vanilli partner Fabrice "Fab" Morvan: "I'm feeling tremendous pain and sorrow upon hearing the news of my friend and brother Rob. He will always be a part of me. We grew up struggling, then succeeding. The only thing we wanted was a chance to sing and perform."

Who could have guessed Milli Vanilli would become an award-winning sensation? No one. But all the success, the money, and recognition meant nothing because it was all based on a lie.

HOW TO SPEAK THE HARD TRUTH

I believe honesty means being up front and open with people on a personal level. If I observe something uncool or unprofessional about a friend, I have a responsibility to tell my friend about his or her actions.

Saying what's on your mind is important, but *how* you say it is really critical. You can be direct and make an impact — but not hurt someone's feelings. Humor can be a great way to soften the impact of speaking a harsh reality. It also depends on what your point of view is. Sometimes I've had to be brutally honest. There was just no other way, BUT I spoke from a caring point of view. I've had people tell me tough truths, but I knew they cared about me and were saying it for my own good. So if the criticism doesn't kill you (and it won't), it makes you stronger.

To go through life pretending that your feelings

don't get hurt, or that you don't care about what other people say to you, is not the way to be successful in life. Not at all.

At all times, keep in the forefront of your mind how you want to be treated and how you want to be spoken to. That's a good indicator for how you should treat other people.

You become a danger to yourself, and society, when you bury your feelings and act on the surface like you don't get hurt. When that happens, people start to act out and become violent and do very destructive things. That's what happens when feelings get buried so deep.

When you have to share a difficult truth with a friend at school or work, think of speaking the truth in love. Whenever possible, build a bridge of trust between yourself and others when times are smooth. That way, when you have something difficult to say, whomever you speak with will know it's because you care.

REAL STORIES

Vocal Ceasing: A Futuristic Story

Strange things were happening aboard the starship *Concordance.* A dangerous virus had infected the computer's communication mode. The computer had begun to respond on its own. The ship's computer team was hard at work looking for the infected component. In the meantime this is what was happening throughout the infected vessel:

Under-captain [Jana] entered his cabin. "Tama," he said to his computer, "install progress report to Nyka quadrant."

"Installing," the computer replied. A section of the wall opened, exposing a large telemonitor. A series of multicolored rolling images unfolded before the officer as the Nyka galaxy appeared, a tiny blip moving among the stars.

"So," the computer spoke, "how long are you going to ignore the inappropriate behavior going on on this ship? This crew is not performing up to capacity. Records are sloppy, and the social deck is a breeding ground for bacteria because the maintenance droids are not kept up to specs."

"I'm not the High Commander of this ship. I

only have so much authority. These people are my friends," the Under-captain said.

"What is your point?" the computer replied. "You know what's going on. It's gone on longer than it should. You are not doing them any favors. Speak up or they're out of here when we get to Nyka. And, sir, you need to go the ship's tailor or spend more time in the workout combat room."

"Computer," the officer said, "cease vocal."

"Vocal ceasing," the computer relied, "but it doesn't change a thing."

M104 sat crying at her station on the engineering deck. "Stop sniveling," the computer said. "You cheated on the exam. You had friends who knew you cheated and none of them said anything. What was I supposed do?"

"I am qualified for this position," M104 said.

"Are you sure? If you had gotten the promotion, you would have been left unsupervised to work with me. You got the answers right but not because you knew them for yourself. I am a very complex system and, frankly, I didn't want to be left alone with you."

"I had to take some time to do some things that were very important to me."

"Your choice. Now don't mess up or you won't have a chance to take the test again. Give me an authorized command."

"I know my job," M104 said, blowing her nose.

"Whatever," the computer replied. "Give me an authorized command."

"Computer, cease vocal."

"Command accepted. Vocal ceasing."

Dana and Rocknar had been kissing since eighteenth level. They both looked forward to a romantic evening. When they got to Rocknar's cabin, the doors would not open. He spoke into the computer's corridor communicator, "Computer, open doors."

"Rocknar," the mechanical voice said, "have you told Dana you have no intention of continuing this relationship, such as it is, once the ship gets to Nyka?"

Dana looked at Rocknar in shock. "What?" she said, almost unable to speak.

"Wake up, Dana," the computer said. "The man's decent as an officer. But he stinks as a friend. He will dump you like an intergalactic potato. Go to your cabin, cry for an hour, take a shower and a couple of aspirin, and thank me in the morning."

Dana turned without a word and went down the corridor.

The doors to the cabin slid open.

"Shame on you," the computer said as Rocknar entered his cabin.

"Computer, cease vocal."

"It's for your own good. Vocal ceasing."

The computer team concluded that it was sabotage. It took them several hours to identify what they called the "hard truth" chip. Their report stated, "It was probably the work of the Teradrians in an attempt to disrupt the harmony on the *Concordance.*"

In the end, the Under-captain went to the High Commander for advice on how to speak to his friends. After all, their jobs were in jeopardy.

M104 signed up for tutoring to prepare for the next exam.

Rocknar's sexual indiscretions were noted and he was transferred to be High Commander of a prison ship destined for the Alpha Pit.

And though her feelings were hurt, Dana concentrated on her work and had a long talk with her mother.

I hope you'll be honest with your friends because, well, there are no computers to help us out. I understand that your friend may get mad at you, call you all kinds of names, and even cut you off for a while. But if your friend knows that you care, he or she will be back. Otherwise, you'll find a good time to approach them and renew your friendship if it's meant to be.

In the meantime, *don't gossip*! Keep your friend's problems — or your problems with your friends — to yourself. This will be hard, but do it. Don't make it possible for something you say to be misunderstood and blown out of proportion. Personally, I feel that if I am inclined to talk to another person, that's talking behind my friend's back. I can't and won't do that and still be able to call myself that person's friend.

My friends have been honest with me. Sometimes, the truth really hurts — like some medicine tastes nasty — but it's always meant to make you feel better.

A LIE IS A LIE

Somebody's always asking you to lie: "Tell them I'm not home." "Tell them I'm in the shower." "Tell them I'm out." A wise man once said, "If I won't lie for you, I won't lie to you."

You can get into trouble for telling the truth. The truth hurts and can rub people the wrong way, especially if they are exposed as a cheater or a liar. Nobody likes to be exposed.

To stand up to authority for what is right — especially if that authority is a parent or guardian — can be scary. It's probably scarier to stand up to your best friend about lying for him or her. What if your best friend just spent time after school at a guy's house "to study" and she asks you to say she was with you? Would it be hard to say no? It happens. If it's already happened with you, how did you respond, and did you have a backup plan if the truth were to come out? One lie often leads to another. Have you asked somebody to cover for you while you went off to do something you know you'd get in trouble for? And the friend who lied for you, what makes you so sure she won't lie to you?

Everyone lies and it's no big deal until someone gets hurt, or a reputation gets smeared.

Don't take the chance; it's not worth it. Just because everybody does it, doesn't make it right or right for you.

"Lying is no big thing. It's not a crime. Anyway, look at the 'big people' who lied, for example, our president, Bill Clinton. He kind of makes it easy for kids to lie today and think they will get away with it." — Steve

"You do pay a price when you are not honest. When you don't tell the truth and you are found out, you don't have the trust of your parents and friends, and your relationships may not be as stable as they were before." — Tasha

"People say everybody lies because they want to lie. That gives them a good excuse to lie. It's not that they don't know better. It is just hard sometimes to tell the truth, so I use the excuse that everybody lies. Some people are very honest. It may be hard to find them but they are out there." — Francisca

3

"Money makes you do things you would never do to get it." — Devin

"You have to be a survivor. We have to get what we need one way or the other." — Jennifer

I began my career at New York Hospital as a medical social worker counseling terminally ill patients and their families. I trained at the hospital for a year and was then hired for around $20,000 a year — not much money, even in those days.

Throughout college and graduate school, I worked at Graham Windham Services for Families and Children, a residential treatment center for emotionally disturbed youth in Hastings-on-Hudson, New York. Over the years, working with troubled youth and the terminally ill took its toll and I became disenchanted with social work as a profession. I took a lot of the issues home with me. Although I knew I could make a difference in some people's lives, I knew there were many things I couldn't change — and that became depressing.

So I began to think about what else I could do. I knew I wanted to make as much money as I could in this lifetime — legally! I also knew it wasn't going to happen in social work.

Then I read an article about a six-week public relations course. It intrigued me for some reason. (Destiny? I didn't know anyone in the field.) I signed up, and the course exposed me to some guest teachers who whetted my appetite and compelled me to take another course. After the course, I knew I wanted a career in public relations.

Soon I decided to do volunteer work to get hands-on PR and marketing experience I could put on my résumé. I started helping friends who were jazz musicians and couldn't afford to hire a PR person. I also worked with nonprofit organizations that had fund-raisers to promote but couldn't afford to hire a PR person. Eventually, my résumé started to reflect my public relations experience.

I was motivated to make a lot of money, but I knew that wasn't all there was to life. I worked at three different organizations and even though public relations was not my primary responsibility, I made it part of my job. I was the program administrator for the Black Filmmaker Foundation and for a black media trade organization after that. I publicized everything that we worked on just so I could get the experience. I worked on developing relationships, giving 110 percent and then some, and doing my best wherever I worked, no matter what I was paid.

Since I've been in public relations, I have represented many of the world's most talented and visible personalities. My general observation of public personae is that, as much money and material goods as they have, a lot of their souls are empty. Many are afraid to be who they really are. They fear that being open about who they are and their personal preferences might reduce their commercial success. For example, a person's marital status may be hidden or camouflaged for the sake of great commercial appeal.

The Benjamins are powerful. You can lose your soul if you pursue them in a way that means you can't truly be who you are.

The Benjamins buy stuff. Toys. A Mercedes-Benz. Fine jewelry. Expensive clothes. A good time. Status. There are ways you can make a lot of money really fast and have all the toys you want, all the parties you want. But lives are destroyed as a result. Sometimes even yours. Greed kills — people, dreams, even past successes.

After the amazing success of *Rocky*, Sylvester Stallone started making sequels left and right. It seemed he wasn't picking his shots carefully and was thinking that all he needed to do was put out the films, and he became less concerned with the final quality of his projects. He also reportedly had a habit of treating people unfairly and eventually he was unable to land good roles.

John D. Rockefeller owned Chevron, Exxon, Shell, and other large companies. He was a wealthy and greedy man, and the public became so fed up with him owning everything but helping nobody that he finally had to hire a public relations firm to repair his image in the public's mind.

You can want something so much you can taste it. You can see it in front of you as plain as day. You're just motivated by what you see. Step-by-step. And each step you mark as a signpost of achievement. You are one step closer. Then you come to the hard part of the journey. It is a dense and rocky forest. You have to get through it and that's where your ambition and your desire to succeed are put to the test. Will you back down and say, "I've done enough," or do you go on? You decide to put the pedal to the metal and take off. Inside, you feel like you're in a hundred-mile-an-hour car chase. But you maintain control because you know where you're going.

In your hand you have a double-edged sword called ambition. You wield it carefully because your blade is sharp. One side of the blade opens a pathway through the forest. The other side of that blade, if you're not careful, will cut people down along the way. But no matter how thick or pliable the branches of the trees in the forest are, you keep moving through it, gaining strength from your ambition and drive.

When you get to that thing you wanted so badly, what does the pathway look like behind you? It's crooked and uneven and you're sweating like a pig, but have you left injured, battered folks along the way? Or are there folks squarely behind you, ready to support you as you head toward the next thing? Greed and ambition are different sides of desire.

I am impressed with the values I hear from many young people regarding money and ambition.

"All I really need is to be financially stable. I don't need to be a millionaire. I just need to be able to support a family when I decide to start one, be able to take my family on trips. I just need enough to live a simple life. That's it." — Andre

"I don't think you should keep on running after money. If you keep running after money, money will become your basis of survival. If you become bankrupt and don't have money anymore, how will you survive? So when all your money is gone, what will you do? So you shouldn't go after money because that will become all that you are living for, to have money." — Stella

"Money isn't everything. Happiness and inner peace are much more important and they don't come from money. These come from who you are. I know this kid who says he is a Christian. I know his family, too. They don't have much money but he's cool. He seems happy." — Kim

Let's face it, money is important. It provides the means for food, clothing, and shelter — the basics. Most people want to be financially independent, or at least to be able to take care of themselves and their family and to live a meaningful life. Money also provides for luxuries such as gourmet food, designer clothes, and a home by the water. Having money isn't bad.

The motivational speaker Zig Ziglar said this: "Money is not everything . . . but it's reasonably close to oxygen. And money will buy me a lot of things: a. a house — but not a home; b. a bed — but not a good night's sleep; c. a companion — but not a friend; d. a good time — but not peace of mind. And I want all those things — and they will only be achieved when you go through life righteously."

But money can easily become more important than the people in your life, peace of mind, caring, loving, laughing, praying, and having a good time. When that happens, you have a problem.

REAL STORIES

Three Hours Before Sunset

Hi, my name is Sandra. I never thought making a little extra money could be, like, dangerous.

This is what happened. Our high school International Club had an old-fashioned car wash. The owner of a closed-down gas station let us hook up the hoses and we stood out on the street with a sign, waving down customers. We washed a lot of cars that day and it was really a lot of fun. My best friend Stacey and I were partners and the two of us were smokin'. We could do a car in no time flat. And our customers went away happy. I just loved accepting their money and getting those tips. A lot of the kids turned in their tips, but we were told we could keep them if we wanted to. I kept mine. Stacey did, too. A girl after my own heart.

So anyway, that afternoon we raised a lot of money for the Foreign Students Dollars for Scholars program.

At about four o'clock, our school counselor, Ms. Klein, announced that we had surpassed the goal and we were free to go home after we had cleaned up all the equipment. That's when I got my bright idea. *Sandra,* I thought to myself, *there are at least three hours of daylight left. There is still time to make more money. If I can get Stace to stay with me, and if we wash ten more cars at seven dollars per car, we'll make seventy dollars! That's thirty-five dollars each.*

I told Ms. Klein that Stacey and I would take care of all the washing stuff — hoses, cleansers, sponges, the whole nine yards. At first Stacey was shaky but when she thought about that extra thirty-five dollars in her pocket, she came around. I made sure we used a Foreign Students League Dollars for Scholars sign because I knew that no one would stop for just a couple of girls with hoses and sponges. People need to feel that they're contributing to a good cause. Stacey made a stink about it; she said it was lying but, well, we didn't say anything that was a lie, we just kept the sign. So I did the flagging.

We got customers. We were fast and efficient. We made more than seven dollars a car because people would give us extra for the good cause. It felt so good to put that money in the coffee can. It was all I could do not to say, "I told you so."

We were doing just fine. By 7:30 we had close to sixty dollars in the can. We would easily beat our

10 P.M. curfew and our parents didn't have to know we were still washing cars instead of going to the movies and pizza.

Then the weird van pulled up. I didn't flag them, they just drove in. The guys inside were asking us how much to do the van. Stacey was standing behind me and she pinched me hard in the back. But she didn't have to because I got this really creepy feeling. I was sure they were smoking pot and one of the guys had a 40-ounce beer in his hand. Stacey said we were just starting to get ready to go home. That's when one of the guys flashed twenty dollars and said if we did a good job it would be ours. Then another guy pulled out another ten-dollar bill and said he'd add that on if we were quick.

My heart was beating really fast. We would beat our goal *and* go for pizza! I was just about to say okay when Stacey grabbed my wrist. I saw her push the remote to unlock the doors of her car and she pulled me to her car. I was running and stumbling at the same time. I didn't know the girl was that strong. I screamed, "The money!"

She said, "Forget the money. Get in here!" I had never heard her be so commanding before and I just did as I was told. As I got in the car, I saw the guys had gotten out of the van and were moving fast in our direction. Stacey gunned the engine and took off swerving. She almost lost control of the car and that scared me. By the time we got to our neighborhood, I was so mad at her. I know I could have handled the situation if we had just stayed calm.

The next day, early before breakfast, I got my brother to take me back. I swore him to secrecy and paid him ten bucks. I was kinda hoping the guys hadn't taken the can with the money. Yeah, right. All the car-washing stuff was still there, but it was like thrown around all over the place. My brother watched while I got everything and put it in the trunk.

I didn't speak to Stacey for a couple of days after that. I never told my parents about what happened. And as far as I know, my brother didn't snitch. But I think Stacey told hers because yesterday at breakfast, my mom said, "If you were ever in trouble, you'd tell us, wouldn't you?" And Dad said, "We love you. You know that, don't you?"

Mom said, "Stacey's mother wondered why you two haven't been hangin' out together, so she gave us a call. We'd really like to hear about the car wash."

I poured the syrup on my waffles and that's when I told them about what had happened Saturday.

You need money for CDs, the movies, the clothes you want to wear that your parents won't buy, time out with your friends, presents, and so forth.

Sandra, the storyteller, had entrepreneurial instincts. That's great ambition. But her greed led to dishonesty because she decided to earn extra money pretending to be fund-raising. You know ambition is turning to greed when something wrong or potentially harmful to yourself or others is involved.

Stacey was conscious of doing wrong, but she was lured by the prospect of additional money in her pocket. She and Sandra did all right for a while. But they ended up in what could have been a very tragic circumstance.

You can go along for a time making money, but eventually you may start to notice you don't have anything else in your life *except* work. You may not have a van full of potentially dangerous guys come up on you, but you might have suffering grades, loneliness, or no really close relationships. A good babysitter can work a lot and make a decent amount of money. People are willing to pay well to know their children are in responsible care. To top it off, if your reputation is good, you can work all the time no matter what kind of work you do. I encourage you, though, to leave time in life for social and after-school activities. If you look up and you're baby-sitting all the time it could begin a pattern in your life that will not be good in the long run.

Let's say you are very ambitious and aspire to be the most in-demand baby-sitter. Consider what it's going to cost you. How many weekends and evenings during the week are you willing to give up? We are not only talking money here; we are talking time. Time you could be spending getting to know your family and friends better, getting to know your boyfriend/girlfriend better, or devoted to your homework.

Have you heard the old saying, "Time is money"? To make a lot of money, you have to put in a lot of time. Balance your time.

So the Benjamins can come two ways — the good way, from ambition, or the bad way, from greed.

Go ahead. Earn money in an honest way with work that is balanced with play and people. Save it, and spend it wisely.

In the book *Having Our Say,* the Delany sisters, Sarah and Bessie, both of whom lived to be over one hundred years old, tell of their father's advice regarding money. "For every dollar you earn, ten cents goes to the Lord [the biblical practice of giving a tithe — 10 percent of your income — to God], ten cents goes in the bank for hard times, and you better be careful how you spend the rest. Well it's a good thing we listened 'cause we're living on that hard time money now."

There are many people who have made and are continuing to make a lot of money. But instead of hoarding it all for themselves, they are doing some wonderful things. For instance, they give to organizations whose goals are to help and enrich humanity. Ted Turner, of Turner Broadcasting, has given one billion dollars to the United Nations to be used over ten years for such causes as fighting disease, helping refugees, and cleaning up land mines. Bill Gates of Microsoft has set up an endowment of $11.3 billion for public libraries to buy, among other things, computers. And noted entrepreneur, civic leader, and Atlanta native Herman J. Russell, Sr., chairman of H.J. Russell & Company, donated $1 million each to Tuskegee University, Clark Atlanta University, Morehouse College, and Georgia State University to expand their programs in entrepreneurship. The four million dollar pledge is the largest gift to entrepreneurship by an African-American in the nation's history.

My former client, Chris Rock, the phenomenally successful comedian and producer of *The Hughleys,* has won a truckload of awards including a Grammy and several Emmys. He could have stopped there, but he hasn't. He is helping to develop other young black comedy writers by launching a humor magazine at Howard University. Just as Harvard University's *National Lampoon* launches the careers of many young writers, Chris's magazine will give young black writers a place to practice their craft before they enter the profession. Now this may not seem very exciting, but the voice of the comic can be very influential. One day you may be laughing at the material of a new comic whose skill was honed while writing for the publication started by Chris Rock. He has a successful career himself in comedy, and now he's sharing the financial rewards.

WHAT BRINGS YOU JOY?

"They say thousands of dollars are being spent in public schools today and look what a mess they are in. I don't know: Something just seems to be missing in life for so many kids and I don't think it is money. — Hunter

"When you want to fit in, you have to wear Tommy Hilfiger and other name brands like that or you might get dissed by others. But I don't care. I wear what I want. I was taught it is who you are, not what you have, money, clothes and stuff like that, that matters." — Jodi

"It isn't all about money, but knowing yourself and what you want and what is important to you. I think about family, friends, doing well in school, and stuff like that. If I continue to do well in school and can get a job I will get some money, but I am not going to focus on money alone." — Maya

"Some people think money is more important than it is. My mother's friend told me about a time when she was growing up that they didn't have any money for anything hardly and she grew up and became somebody. That's what I think about. Sure, I would I like to have more money and I do think it is important to have money for things, but I am thinking more about going to college and making something of myself." — Ruthie

Often, the parents of famous people say they saw the seeds of greatness when their children were little. I often see how professional basketball players act around fans and I've noticed something very compelling about the way Terrell Brandon, NBA All-Star point guard, interacts with young children. Sometimes players don't even look at kids when they are signing autographs, but Terrell has a special way of dealing with them. He literally stops what he is doing to be with that kid at that time.

Charlotte Brandon, Terrell's mother and founder of Mothers of Professional Basketball Players, is proud of the man he has become — talented, of course, but also a *genuine* person. She saw these qualities in him when he was growing up; he exemplified kindness and always considered other people. At three and a half years old, his mother remembers him getting on the bus to go to preschool and helping the bus driver escort the girls onto the bus, making sure they had a seat. "It was because he saw his father give respect," she says. He was always very sensitive toward people who had disabilities and it bothered him whenever people took advantage of them. These things start young, according to Charlotte.

Shirley Garnett, mother of Kevin Garnett of the Minnesota Timberwolves, who is also an NBA All-Star, a member of the 2000 U.S. Olympic Dream

Team, and was featured on the cover of *Sports Illustrated* as one of today's premier players, says that during Kevin's junior high school years he was an all-star player, but she didn't know he was playing basketball. She did not give him permission to play because she was worried about his getting an education. Kevin tells people that no one's mother was stricter than his; she wouldn't accept poor grades. He loved basketball so much that he got a friend to sign the permission slip. He kept up with his grades so his mother wouldn't know he was playing.

One day the school bus arrived at her house and there was no Kevin. She got in the car and went to the school. There were a lot of cars parked in the front, and she had to park far away. As she got closer to the school, she heard noise from the gymnasium. She thought he had stayed after school for a pep rally. She told the security guard at the gym she was looking for her son, Kevin, and the security guard told her Kevin couldn't come out because he was on the court. Shirley was dumbfounded, having no idea her son played basketball. She went into the gym and it was packed. Kevin was playing hard, the crowd shouting "Kevin, Kevin" as he dribbled and dunked. That is when Shirley realized her son could play basketball and that it was his destiny. From then on she was at every game.

Rita Owens, Queen Latifah's mother, says she saw seeds of greatness in her daughter when Dana was in the sixth grade. She sang "Home" as Dorothy from *The Wiz* and received a standing ovation. The audience was captivated, giving her the only standing ovation of the evening. Rita's brother had come from out of town to see Dana, and even he had tears in his eyes after the performance. Rita knew then that her daughter was going to be great.

If these parents could see something in these celebrities when they were kids, it means those kids were already beginning to reach for their dreams. So, your daydreams are important. What do you envision yourself doing? Even if it sounds silly, there is a reason why it appeals to you. What makes you feel really alive? Do you find yourself reading everything you can about a certain subject? Your fascination could be more than just curiosity; it may be your purpose in life, the way you'll earn your Benjamins in the future.

An interesting exercise is to step outside yourself and observe how you behave in different situations. When you feel most happy, what are you doing?

K-K Gregory is a fifteen-year-old entrepreneur.

She was featured on *Oprah* along with others who had started their own businesses. K-K designed a fleece fingerless glove called Wristies that protects the wrist from the cold yet leaves the fingers free. She started out making them for her Girl Scout troop. But the kids really liked them and told her she could make money. And she has.

In *The Young Entrepreneur's Guide,* Steve Mariotti describes how a group of angry and belligerent students changed their behavior as they began to learn about math through using business skills. At first they just learned on paper, but soon they began to deal with an actual product. Some went on to start their own small businesses, from selling sunglasses to doing manicures. Mariotti says, "Their challenging lives encouraged independence of spirit, toughness, unself-consciousness, and a natural ability in salesmanship. They were comfortable with risk and ambiguity. These same qualities — along with difficulty in doing well in a traditional, structured environment — characterized such great American entrepreneurs as Henry Ford (automobiles) and Conrad Hilton (hotels)."

Discovering they had an affinity for sales encouraged these students. What do you have a flair for? Do you prefer to be at a party or in your room reading a mystery? When you look at the world do you see what is concrete or do you look at what might be? Do you make your decisions based on facts or feelings? Do you prefer things organized or spontaneous? Knowing even these little things about yourself can be a great asset to you as you grow. You might have artistic strengths you could pursue, as K-K did, through designing or building. When the Benjamins start to come in, it'll be because you were doing what you loved.

Sister Souljah, rap artist and political activist, has written a novel entitled *The Coldest Winter Ever.* The main character, Winter, is at a gathering of about fifty women led by a woman named Souljah. Winter tells readers something that Souljah says,

> *Everybody thinks it's all about the Benjamins, but if every black person in the ghetto received a thousand dollars each in the mail tomorrow, what would happen? Most people got excited at that thought. A bunch of side conversations about what people would do with their thousand jumped off.*
>
> *Souljah said, In one week, 90 percent of our people would be broke. The money would be spent on overpriced jewelry, clothes, liquor, food, and crack. Everybody started laughing.*

True, some of them said.

Now if we could work on who we are, what we stand for, getting to know each other, and what we believe, then we can make better decisions. For example, if everybody in here received a thousand dollars each and we believed in unity, we could have fifty thousand to buy a piece of property or put a down payment on a house, or we could open up a business and all become shareholders. It would be hard work, but at the end of the day it would mean so much more.

Ask yourself, "What is important to me? Is it just about the money?"

It's funny as I look back on my earliest thoughts about what I wanted to do because it was always about helping people and doing my part to save the world. Every single thing I have done — even when I called myself changing careers — has been about helping others.

My agency has represented major corporations as well as sports and political figures. By working with the people in these positions, we get to put them together with various organizations that could benefit from the use of the client's name or resources. We can direct our clients' voices, clout, power, and money into areas that can help a lot of people in significant ways.

I believe the success of the agency stems from my philosophy. We are on this planet to support one another as human beings, first, last, and always. My clients are human beings whom I am here to support. I love it.

What do you love? There *is* a way you can make money doing it. Do what you love and the money will come. You may have a really good idea. Another young girl who was on *Oprah* had a good idea. Her father made bacon in the microwave but was wrestling with the grease. Abbey Fleck, thirteen years old at the time, said, "You could just hang it up." Her dad fiddled with the idea and Makn Bacon was born. They started out with a three-hundred-dollar investment and at airtime they had three million dollars in sales.

Identify what means the most to you in your life. If you could, right at this moment, choose what your future would be like, what would be there? Who would be there? What would you be doing? Now is a good time to think about those things. Don't be afraid to think about the future. Go ahead and dream. For a minute or two forget all the negative things people have said to you about who you are or what you can or cannot achieve.

Do what you love: The Benjamins will come.

How often have you seen a child get a whole lot of stuff for Christmas and play with the boxes rather than the toys? That moment when the imagination takes over is simply magical. Suddenly they have a submarine or cave where they hide from the tickle monster. Don't let the magical moments get by you. When you have that moment of understanding about yourself, your dreams and desires, pay attention. Then ask yourself, "How do I pass this on to others? How do I make a difference in the lives of my family, my friends, and my community?"

I repeat, the money you need will be there. With ambition, not greed and passion, it won't be all about the Benjamins, it will be about ________.

You fill in the blank.

"I think about so many famous people who are miserable. They have all the money in the world, but marry a million times. I bet their kids must be miserable never knowing where they are going to be the next day or who their next mother or father will be." — Mary

"I feel like that sometimes. I don't like to admit it but I am a selfish person sometimes. I don't want to be bothered. I am a loner and like to be by myself and I don't want people bothering me. But when I think that maybe there are people who want someone to talk to them who may not enjoy being by themselves like I do, then I think differently. I think that if I see them and they look sad, maybe I should go out of my way and start to talk to them. You never know how just speaking to someone might cheer them up. Also since I do think I am my brother's keeper in a sense, I guess going out of my way a little bit does say something about how I feel about myself, that maybe I do have something to offer other people more than I thought." — Matthew

There are twenty-four hours in a day. And today we have more than enough to fill that time. First of all, there's school, or school and the job, not to mention homework, meetings, practices, and rehearsals. Then there are friendships, boyfriends, or girlfriends. Perhaps we have major responsibilities to our families. It would be understandable if you just didn't want to be bothered with all the things that press on you. It would be good to not have to deal with a whole lot of stuff. Just the obligations — that's it. The rest of the time you could do your own thing or hang out with your friends.

I confess there are days when I just don't want to be bothered, and it is all I can do to go the *first* mile. I understand that. That's what makes going the extra mile valuable. When you go past what you feel, you can find a miracle just five minutes away.

To give you an example, a screening I did not want to attend (I dragged myself to it) led to my landing Eddie Murphy as my first client. I had heard on a few occasions that Eddie was looking for a publicist. So, I'm at this screening where I don't want to be and during a conversation, an acquaintance says, "I hear Eddie Murphy is looking for a PR person." At that moment I decided to get a package to Eddie. I knew it wasn't coincidence I was hearing it again — I knew I was supposed to represent him. I was exactly where I was supposed to be that night. I was scared to go out on my own but I also had no choice. I was a social worker ready to move on — without the benefit of industry contacts, money, or experience starting a business. That night I was tired and did not feel like being bothered. But that effort resulted in my becoming the first personal publicist for one of the biggest names in the entertainment industry.

In *Personal Touch* I wrote, "I will never forget the night I called over to Eddie's home and was speaking with Ray Murphy, Jr., Eddie's cousin, [and] vice president of production at Eddie Murphy Productions . . . before Ray and I had the opportunity to really start talking, he said, 'Hold on a second, Terrie. Eddie's here and wants to talk to you.'

"I gotta tell you, when Eddie Murphy, the number-one box-office champion, one of the most recognizable stars in the world, got on the phone and said, 'I got your package, and I would love to have you represent me,' I cried. Those were his exact words. I'll never forget them."

Sometimes when we least feel like being bothered is when we should go for it.

Don't Wanna Be There

There's a party goin' on and hey I don't care / I'm feeling right now like don't want to be there / I don't want to be bothered and have to pretend / I know there's gonna be someone I'll prob'ly offend / but they'll have to get over it / let it slide off their back / but I don't want to be bothered and it may sound whack / There are all kinds of things goin' on in my mind that need my attention / and are kind of important to how I make myself be / cause I'm thinkin' a lot about what makes me me / What makes me authentic and genuine / what makes me feel good and what makes my life mine / and all the distractions at home and at school it's hard to just think to chill to be cool / When all o' the pressures around you press on and press in / and make you to think I don't like where I've been / and I know that I need to go somewhere new / but I need time to think / to go out to the edge / and be in space / where my life can just get all up / in my face / but when people intrude want my time / and attention / I get kind of angry 'cause I know I can't mention the stuff that is going on inside of me / and makin' me slide and makin' me bend / I don't want to be bothered and don't want to pretend / but later I know I'll give up some of me / to be with you / and for you and not to ignore you / but that will come later at some other time / when I get me some reason and get me some rhyme / but I don't want to be bothered and I know you my friend / but please let me be I don't want to pretend

— Sharita Hunt

THE IMPORTANCE OF FIRST IMPRESSIONS

"That's fake. You put on a front. People think you are something that you really are not. You should just be yourself. Sometimes all of us don't feel like being bothered. But if you just stop and think about it a few minutes, your feelings will probably change because you think about the times somebody was bothered by you." — Stefan

"You shouldn't have to pretend. Just like I don't feel like being bothered right now. So I am saying I don't want to be interviewed right now. Let's talk later, okay. I think that is how you should let people know you don't want to be bothered." — Joel

"Pretending smells. Just be yourself." — Karen

You don't have to pretend to make a good first impression. Ask yourself, "How do you want to come across? Am I going to regret this sour attitude later?" A good sense of humor always works. Ask yourself, "What kind of a person am I?" Behave like the kind of person you are. You'll find that whether or not you want to be bothered just then has little to do with the core of your character.

Another plan of attack is when you don't want to be bothered, just consider the other person rather than yourself. Instead of thinking you have to be fake and please somebody, take into account how you would want to be treated if the other person didn't want to be bothered. That might help guide you and relieve some of the stress.

When you meet people in professional situations, always give a firm handshake — your full hand, not just fingers. Look them in the eye. Speak so you are heard and understood. Smile! Research studies show that people who smile are perceived as more intelligent than people who don't. So when I say "smile when you meet people and give a firm handshake," I'm not talking about being phony. I'm just talking about putting your best foot forward.

How you present yourself to others will vary depending on your dress and grooming. But whomever you are with, keep yourself clean. If you only have one shirt, take care of it. Appearance is part of making an impression and good grooming makes the people you meet feel comfortable.

There are going to be times when you just don't want to be bothered doing some of those things. You won't always be perfect because none of us is, but when the best outweighs the mediocre, that is what will follow you.

True friends will understand when you are not your best self. They know more facets of you and your personality. But someone you meet for the first time doesn't know you. Before your initial encounter with someone you do not know, ask yourself how you want them to remember you. Act on that.

When I originally thought of the importance of first impressions, I was thinking of the impression we make on others when meeting for the first time. But there is another angle — the impression we *receive* when we meet someone for the first time. It's a very interesting dilemma. It is easy to jump to conclusions and be very wrong about someone, just as there are times when you are misjudged. I know there are times when I am "no day at the beach" and I wouldn't want you to hold it against me. Though you have control over how you present yourself, reserve your thoughts about others. If you cut them some slack, and you get to know them better, you'll be glad you did not judge them too harshly from the jump.

REPUTATION IS ALL YOU HAVE

A while ago I had two clients who did something that was not cool. Both incidents had to do with photo shoots. The first was scheduled for 9 A.M. at his summer home, at his request. He didn't show up until 4:45 P.M., arriving by helicopter. In the meantime, the crew had left New York City at 4 A.M. to be on time for the 9 A.M. shoot.

The other person was six hours late for a photo shoot. He walked in with no apology, had an attitude, was not cooperative, and gave the magazine only a half hour for the shoot.

These are very gifted people, but they were developing a reputation for not being reliable or cooperative. While that may be "acceptable" behavior when they are on top, when the careers start to fade, as careers often do, people won't want to be bothered or give them the benefit of the doubt.

Reputation is all you have. A good reputation is like a plant. In order for a plant to grow properly and thrive, it must be watered, fed, and given the right amount of light depending on the kind of plant it is. What is sure to kill a plant is lack of care. The same goes for your reputation. You take care of your reputation in the ways that you deal with people and with the tasks you encounter as you move through this world. Nurturing your reputation is a day-to-day activity. As a young person, now is a good time to start taking care of your reputation.

Why would you want to be bothered? So many desires and wishes can be just outside your reach.

But it doesn't have to stay like that. There are ways to deal with all the pressures that make you feel like not being bothered.

"A good reputation and respect are worth much more than silver and gold." — Proverbs 22:1

TALKING HEALS

My friend tells me the story of the New Year's Eve her father was cooking chitlins. Chitlins are pig guts — that's right. Chitlin comes from the word chitterling, which is like a ruffle down the front of a shirt or blouse and is an accurate description of what pig guts look like. Chitlins are very tough and take hours over a flame to cook. (People tell me such things, since the only things I use in my kitchen are the microwave and the refrigerator. In twenty years I have never used my dishwasher. But that's another story.) My friend's father cooked them in a pressure cooker, which takes less than half the time. He used the stove in the basement to cook them (they can smell pretty funky). He lost track of time and got involved in something else on the first floor. There was a loud boom. My friend heard it in her bedroom on the second floor. The pot had exploded, the lid had blown off and split in two when it hit the concrete basement floor. There were pig guts hanging from the ceiling and all over the floor and walls.

Fortunately no one was hurt, but pressure cookers tend to be made of heavy steel and there could have been a serious injury.

When you use a pressure cooker, there is a valve you have to watch, or the top blows off. When it gets to a certain point, you turn off the heat. Then you can let the cooker sit for a few minutes until the valve stops moving or you can run cool water over the pot to bring the temperature down.

Sometimes our lives put a lot of pressure on us. There is also a way to control those pressures in our lives. Talking to a trusted friend or adult can be just like sitting off to the side and gently blowing off steam — or like having cool water calm you down.

We can't always repair damage; but we can always recover. The lessons we learn from missteps build character.

Talk about the things that make you afraid, angry, or disappointed. You've got to *really* want to conquer them though — because it's much easier said than done. Communicate with your parents, or the counselor at school, or another adult you consider a friend. You might even ask to spend some time with a professional counselor or therapist. Sometimes people think it's weird or you gotta be crazy to talk to a counselor. I consider it a gift to have that opportunity. Call me crazy, then.

I know it's hard, but talking things out can help you to see various points of view. Your parents or a counselor will be able to ask you questions or suggest ideas you had not considered. In a way it's like the difference between seeing a piece of clothing on a hanger and on your body. Some things look really bad on the hanger, but when you put them on it's a totally different vibe.

Also, when we talk to people, we find out we're not alone. If one person has experienced it, you can be sure many others have experienced it, too. One of the reasons support groups work so well is that they allow you to identify others who have the same problem. You hear somebody else talking and you could swear it's you. Members help one another find ways to cope that work and last. You don't have to feel alone anymore. Someone else has walked the path before you.

Another way to sort through the tough stuff is to write down what you're feeling and thinking. Then set it aside for a couple of days before you go back to it. Does it still make sense? Do you have any new understanding about what you wrote? A journal can be a big help.

Problems are a part of life and we all have to deal with them. Everybody has bad days. It's how we respond to them that makes the difference. But if you find your bad days are turning into weeks, talk to someone whom you trust — even if they don't necessarily agree with you, they will respect your feelings and will be there to support you. Talking can be a major step toward healing. Even if you don't want to be bothered.

BUT, TERRIE, I REALLY DON'T WANT TO BE BOTHERED!

Having said so much about making impressions, building a good reputation, and talking things out, now I can say, "Don't do anything you really don't want to do when you really can't be bothered." Be polite with your "no" and pass. It's better you're not there because if your attitude is messed up it will spoil things for you and everyone else. You have to take time off to replenish your energy. If you truly don't feel like being bothered, the best thing for you to do is politely and respectfully decline or excuse yourself. You can always do it with sincerity or humor. I know when I am tired and someone asks me to do something, I often say, "I am so tired I can't do it for $100,000 a day and free food." It's gotten easier for me to say no to things if I honestly feel I can't do them — because I've come to understand that saying no is a vote of yes for me.

When you're dealing with a friend and don't feel like being bothered, in a polite way suggest another time that would be better. If possible, be specific. For example, "I can't right now, but how about in an hour?" or "I can't talk right now, but I'll call you at 6:30, okay?" If it's not a close friend or it's someone with whom you really don't want to spend time, a simple and polite, "Thank you, but I can't," without making excuses, should do it.

If someone does not understand that you have chosen not to participate and you were considerate in how you spoke, then that's their issue and you can feel good about yourself. You must be good to yourself — and remember that you can't be your best self and give to others if you're not right with yourself first. If you start extending yourself beyond what is healthy, you will begin to show signs of self-neglect. And it will come out in ways that can be very destructive. You can't do anything for anyone else unless you take care of yourself. It's taken me a long time to learn this.

Other times you just have to suck it up and put forth the best possible face or vibe — be bothered even though you don't want to be. People are always watching — and you never know how your energy will impact someone. There are times when you just have to do something for a friend or a loved one because it's the right thing to do. And then there are times when it is an issue of right and wrong. You must decide to be bothered, take courage, and step up to the plate. When Rosa Parks refused to give up her seat on a bus, she changed the course of history in this country. President Nelson Mandela, imprisoned for twenty-seven years, was offered his freedom and refused, altering the direction of a country. Albert Einstein wrote in his essay, "The World As I See It,"

"A hundred times every day I remind myself . . . that I must exert myself in order to give in the same measure as I have received."

Be bothered. Be real in your pursuits and in your relationships with other people. You can make a difference.

"I have had stuff happen to me as a child, my dad and all, but I do have some pride in myself. I have been able to do well — well, pretty well — in school even though my dad is not at home. My mom works hard for us and I want someday to help her out. Maybe sometimes she felt like she did not want to be bothered with me but I am glad she did." — Tatyana

"Talking is your business — and you are in business to grow." — Xavier Artis, spoken word artist

How you talk *is* your business. The words you choose to use are your business, too. You decide if you want people to understand what you're saying. You decide whether you want to be heard.

What if everyone spoke to each person they met any way they pleased — in slang, scientific terms, religious terms, profanity, even a foreign language, and it didn't matter. Can you imagine never understanding someone when they spoke to you? What if you didn't know what certain slang words or phrases meant? That would be very frustrating. In the final analysis, everybody would be talking just the way they pleased, but no one would really communicate.

We speak to express ourselves, but we want to be heard and understood; otherwise there's not much point. When I was growing up I was always mindful of incorrect grammar, even with my friends. I'm a natural teacher, I guess, and in working with young people and guiding their careers, I've always tried to show them the right way to say things.

TALKING SLANG

"Most teens are bilingual. Kids talk in a certain code language. They feel like they need to be different. The way I talk is the way all kids talk. Sometimes we don't want the adults to know what we are talking about so we talk in our codes. I am sure adults use code language so we don't get it. Adults can be right by us and don't know what we are talking about." — Reggie

Having your own language gives a special sense of community, a bond between you and your friends and the teenage culture at large. In fact, throughout the decades, every generation has had its own form of communication. You get all the nuances and slang in rap songs that your folks are clueless about and probably hate. You can speak in such a way that even when adults are around we don't have the slightest idea what's going on. It's been that way for a long time.

Just as you use your language to draw people in,

you can use it to keep people at a distance. Be careful of using words and phrases so full of slang that you give the message "you are not one of us" or "I am not interested in you enough to speak in a way I know you'll understand." It's just rude.

Using good grammar — the rules of standard English — and words everyone understands allows you to communicate with others across barriers of personality, region, class, or ethnic origin. You are stronger when you are able to communicate with anyone. So, enjoy your slang, but know when *not* to use it.

REAL STORIES

Phat or Fat

Rocky couldn't believe it. His Aunt Josephine was in town singing at the Opera House. It had even been advertised on the radio that Josephine Floyd, the astounding mezzo-soprano, was going to be singing the title role in the opera *Carmen,* by some guy named Bizet.

Aunt Josephine wanted the family to come the second night so that afterward they could all be

together. That was so cool. She wanted to be with her family. So after the performance all the family gathered at the house. His mom had fixed some really tasty hors d'oeuvres and her favorite punch with ginger ale, fruit punch, sherbet, and because it was a special occasion, champagne. He thought Mom and Dad were unreasonable not letting him have any, but since he was going to be sixteen soon and getting his driver's license, he decided to pick his battles. Drinking champagne was not a high priority.

Everybody looked really good in their gowns and tuxedos. He was impressed with how good Maia looked. He noticed she had really nice skin. He thought of her as a cousin because she was part of the family, but was glad they were not blood relatives. He thought he'd ask her to dance later and hold her close. He grinned to himself as he passed the mirror in the hall. He thought he looked good. He hoped Aunt Josephine would think so, too.

"What's she like?" his little cousin Becky asked.

Rocky had not seen Aunt Josephine in years. "The only thing I remember about her is that she smelled good and laughed a lot," he said. He remembered her laugh was kind of funny. It started high and ha-haed down the scale like she was doing a singing exercise. She did that a lot in the opera. Boy, she was a really good singer.

He could not wait to tell her how much he liked what she did. He didn't understand everything, and didn't particularly like everything, but he wanted to tell her how cool she was.

The doorbell rang and everybody got quiet hoping it would be her. And it was. When Aunt Josephine stepped into the room, everyone clapped and she took a small bow. Her man and her manager followed her in and she immediately introduced them to the family.

Josephine hugged her sister, his mom, and you could tell they really loved each other. Then she hugged all the other sisters. He thought it was so amazing that she had come to their house instead of making them go to a restaurant or something like that.

"She's pretty, huh?" little Becky said.

"Yeah. She is," Rocky agreed. Rocky and Becky sat together and talked until they could tell that all the important relatives had had their time with Aunt Josephine.

When it looked like a good time, Rocky and Becky walked up to Aunt Josephine, who was surrounded by her sisters.

"Aunt Josephine," little Becky said with confidence, "Rocky and me think you are so phat!"

All the surrounding sisters gasped! And the minute that followed could only be described as something the Tasmanian Devil could get down with.

"Rebecca Maxine Ward," Aunt Liz said, "you apologize right this minute."

"But Aunt Liz —" Rocky started to speak but was cut off.

"Mama —" Confused, Becky started to speak and was cut off, too.

The other aunts chimed in. "You know we raised you better than that."

"Oh, Josephine, please, this child knows better and I can't believe she said that. I am so embarrassed," Aunt Liz said.

"Rocky, did you have anything to do with —" Aunt Francine started.

"No, Aunt Fran. Becky just meant —"

"Rosemary," Aunt Elizabeth called. "Come here right now."

Rocky's mom came over. "What's the matter?" she asked.

"Your son is encouraging my little girl to say rude things."

"No, Mamma," Rocky said.

Becky started to cry. Everybody was yelling and making accusations. Rocky picked up Becky who held on tight.

Suddenly, Rocky heard, over all the noise, Aunt Josephine's high-to-low laugh. She stood and walked to Rocky and took little Becky in her arms. She kissed her and said, "Thank you, sweet pea. I think you're really cool, too."

Aunt Josephine looked at Rocky and smiled. "You have grown into a very handsome young man. Let me tell you, that tux is the bomb."

Josephine sat down and started having a conversation with little Becky. Rocky smiled as all the aunts, confused, drifted off to a corner to try and figure out what had just happened.

Rocky couldn't believe the confusion that had erupted all because his aunts didn't know that "phat" meant something good. He felt they should have at least let him explain what Becky had meant. Becky was just a little kid and they jumped all over her. Then he thought, *And they wonder why I don't want to talk to them sometimes. They just lost it. They were out of control. But Aunt Josephine, she* is *the bomb. She knew what Becky was saying.*

Then he took a deep breath, straightened his tie, and went to tell his aunts what was going on.

When people get angry or embarrassed they don't listen very well. And so the aunts made it impossible for Rocky and Becky to explain what they were saying. They jumped to conclusions because they had no idea that *phat* meant something good. All they heard was *fat*; they responded to what they knew. Rocky would probably not have used slang out loud with Aunt Josephine considering she's a big star. Becky, on the other hand, was just a little kid who did not know better.

It's best to use the appropriate language at the right time to avoid misunderstandings.

There is a vocabulary-building product called Verbal Advantage® whose slogan is, "People judge you by the words you use." Unfortunately, people will make a judgment about how smart, educated, or capable you are by the way you use the English language. Have you ever made an assumption about someone based on the way they talk? Right or wrong, we do it.

Go ahead and use slang. It sounds better to you, and your friends understand you. At the same time have command of correct English, ready for those times when you need it.

Using standard English is a must in a lot of different circumstances. For instance, in a job interview there needs to be clear communication between you and the interviewer. If you use slang, the person who interviews you may feel you are not sophisticated enough or educated enough to work for the company — or, worse, that you feel "too good" to speak in terms the interviewer can understand. Standard English is also important in the workplace, where you will have to maintain the company's image and need to be able to communicate with everyone.

Being understood and making others comfortable with your speech is important. When speaking to your whole class you realize everyone may not be one of your crew and they may not understand what you're talking about. It won't do any good if you have a brilliant presentation and your teacher, the one who gives the grade, has no idea what you just said. More than likely the class will laugh *at* you, and the teacher will be disgusted.

And if you want your love interest to say yes when you ask for a date, that person needs to realize you asked to go out!

PROFANITY

I had an experience recently with a temporary employee who is lovely and intelligent. After about a week into her four-week stint as my assistant, she asked me if I'd consider using a little less profanity. She said it made her uncomfortable and she thought my use of such words sometimes filtered into the rest of the office.

At first, I said to myself (and to her in a more diplomatic way), "Well, who does she think she is coming into my house, telling me how I should talk?" Then I thought about it from her point of view and how harsh profanity can sometimes sound. So I said, "You know what? I hear you. And I will make a concerted effort to be mindful of my words, but keep in mind that that is who I am and I am in *my* house." She thanked me. We had a very warm, respectful, and pleasant working relationship — and even laughed often during the month as I worked on censoring my tongue.

I like to cuss, but I do know there are times to curb it. There are times when it is just inappropriate. I'll avoid it out of respect for friends or colleagues who have a distaste for profanity.

People use profanity all the time to address one another or describe one another with friendly intention. While I use profanity — okay, I admit I can talk like a truck driver and I like using certain words that say it like no other word can — I realize that it becomes a habit of communication. You may find you've been a little too free and easy and you could slip up at the wrong time. We have to be willing to take responsibility for the outcome of what we say, how we say it, and the impression it leaves. You could miss out on knowing some great people because of how you speak.

MAKING CONVERSATION

When I worked at New York Hospital after graduate school and before going into public relations, I was the youngest and the only social worker of color in a department of forty workers. At times, I felt inadequate and I wasn't very outgoing. I handled my caseload and at lunchtime I'd go to my small office in the basement of the hospital, eat lunch — every day a hamburger, french fries, and a milk shake — and take a nap.

After a while, I realized that it was really pathetic to be sitting in the office eating a heavy lunch like that and going to sleep. Being afraid to be around people was really ridiculous. People would ask me to go to lunch and I always made an excuse not to go. I decided that as difficult as it would be to go to lunch with someone, I would go. I forced myself to go to lunch with someone once a week. That is how I started to come out of my shell. Part of why I was shy was because I didn't think I had anything to talk about. So, on a cheat sheet I started to jot down little things I had read that I could refer to if there was a block in the conversation.

Make a cheat sheet if you need to, but a simpler method I've learned since is to ask about others. Ask people something about themselves. People like to talk about their lives and jobs or schools. They like to share their experiences.

A resource I use for questions to stimulate thought and conversation is called *A Book of Questions — To Keep Thoughts and Feelings* by William Zimmerman. It's a journal for recording your personal thoughts and feelings. The purpose of the book is to help you get to know yourself better. The questions below aren't too personal to ask in conversation:

- **What have been the happiest times of your life?**
- **What special thing happened to you today?**
- **What's been your most favorite adventure? Why?**
- **What is the greatest experience you've ever had?**
- **When it comes down to it, what do you really believe in?**
- **If you could make a great movie or write a book, what would it be about?**
- **What new land or place would you like to go to?**
- **Who is your favorite artist? Why?**
- **What kind of invention would you like to invent? What would it do?**
- **Who do you admire? Why?**

You can practice with your close friends. Then when you feel comfortable, you can take on the world.

When you ask your questions, consider essay questions like, "What do you think about violence on TV?" which can't be answered simply. Before you start talking about yourself and expressing your opinions, listen to others. Have you ever tried to listen to talk radio? Have you noticed that when people call in to give their opinion on a topic, there is very little communication going on? Most of the time it's people talking. No one hears anyone else. No one is willing to be wrong or corrected. Often the host ends up cutting the caller off — or it ends up being a verbal free-for-all.

Listening is a skill that has to be developed. It's hard to listen because our brains move a lot faster than our ears hear. Whomever you're talking with will know you're listening if you are able to tell them in your own words the essence of what they have just said. If you're on target and understanding, they sense you are feeling what they feel. If you've misunderstood they can clarify. Either way, you win. You can carry on a perfectly good conversation with someone by asking questions and getting them to talk about themselves. People will tell you what a great conversationalist you are and how much they enjoyed talking with you.

Some general rules for conversation are:

- **Be creative — even outrageous — but always appropriate.**
- **Avoid gossip.**
- **Avoid racial or sexual jokes.**
- **Don't comment on physical handicaps.**
- **Don't say anything negative about someone's appearance, date, or family.**
- **Be positive without being phony.**

MAKING INTRODUCTIONS

A quick word about the "mechanics" of introductions. According to Mary Mitchell, a national advice columnist and author of *Dear Ms. Demeanor,* "The correct way to introduce your mother to your teacher is to say, 'Ms. Lammers, I'd like to introduce my mom, Mrs. Kannof.'

"The correct way to introduce your friends to your mother is to say, 'Mom, this is my friend Frank Hales. He sits behind me in school, and we're in the debate club together. Frank, this is my mother, Mrs. Kannof.'"

She goes on to give very good advice. "It helps to give a little information about the people you are introducing so that they will have something to talk about. Don't forget to say your mother's last name, especially if it is different from yours."

Everybody gets befuddled making introductions. If you get all tongue-tied, just say, "Ms. Lammers, this is Mrs. Kannof." Don't worry about which names go first. Go for it. Everybody will appreciate your effort.

When you meet someone who is being introduced to you, here's what you do: Look at the person, smile, shake hands, and say, "Good to meet you."

People will be flattered if you can call them by name after only a brief introduction. Have you ever noticed how you always hear your name above the fray? There can be all kinds of music, laughing, talking, even traffic noise. Even when it's just *close* to your name, you hear it.

Try to develop a way of remembering names. Here is one way you can do it. It's all based on the fact that your recall is best when you *want* to remember, when the words are simple and when you reinforce them with repetition. Here's how: 1. Set your priorities before you meet with a new group of people. Figure out whom you want to meet and why. This will motivate you. 2. If you need to know first names and not last names, or vice versa, concentrate only on the part you need. As you meet each new person, say his or her name aloud. Repeat the name in your head several times as you look at the person.

I was at a meeting where there were several people in public relations. T. Boone Pickens, a very influential man in business, was the speaker. For some reason during the talk, he zeroed in on me and remembered my name. My attention to him after that was unwavering. As far as I can tell there was no reason for him to remember my name but he did. Our names are very important to us. When we hear our name we take notice.

BODY LANGUAGE SPEAKS VOLUMES

"Maybe body language is important, but I sure want to hear the guys say I look fine. They can also give me those sweet looks and then it makes me know that for sure they know who I am. — Brittany

It's good to make yourself more aware of the signals people give off through their bodies. A former intern at my company, Omyra, works as a page at NBC where she gives several tours a day. She pays attention to the body language of the group and gets a feel for how she should proceed with the tour.

So, what if there's someone you really want to talk to, but they seem to be in a really deep conversation with someone else? You check out what their bodies are doing. You see them standing kind of close, focused on each other, maybe even touching — that moment is not the right time to move in and enter the conversation. Just hold out and you'll see an opening. In the meantime, there might be somebody you notice who seems to be alone. You can bring them into the center of things by introducing yourself and then introducing them to someone else. They will really appreciate you helping them in an awkward situation.

You see an opportunity to go and speak with that person you really want to meet or talk to. But watch out for whether their eyes start to wander. If you're getting a lot of those "I see, I see, right, right" with a lot of head nodding, there's a good possibility you should say, "Well, it was good talking with you. Let's stay in touch." And get out of their face.

Now it's not only what you observe, but also what you display. You could be standing in such a way — say have your arms wrapped around yourself — that could say you're not friendly or you don't really want to be in conversation. Then again, you could be casual and relaxed. Your body says, "Here stands a really nice person who is looking for other nice people to get to know and hang with. In fact, I just spotted someone that I bet is pretty interesting."

It is not silly to want to make a positive impression on the people you meet. It's natural to want those of the opposite sex to think you are fine. Your body language says a lot about who you are. If you walk into a room with confidence, others will think you're fine. But understand, your body language might also communicate something that could get you into a position you did not have in mind. You may be smart and thoughtful, but be aware that the way you move when you walk, or toss your hair or earrings, may *not* be interpreted as "Wow, that girl is smart and thoughtful." You may be *saying* one thing — but your body language and eye contact will tell people what you're really feeling.

OVERCOMING SHYNESS

"I feel sometimes that talking is not important. I am a quiet person. But sometimes it is important to talk because that is how you get to know people. You won't know who that person is unless they tell you."
— Meaza

An adage comes to mind: "It is better to keep quiet and be thought a fool than to open your mouth and be known a fool." There's a lot of wisdom in that. I think it is important not to talk just to hear yourself talk, but it is important to say something of substance when you do open your mouth.

Being quiet has the advantage of letting you observe others. But I can't stress enough how much better you feel and how illuminated the world becomes when you do talk with other people.

Lots of people are shy. When people meet well-known personalities, they are often amazed that they are not what they expected. People who are in the limelight step out of themselves to do what they have to do. But there is no difference between a star and a kid who has to go to a new school and meet all new kids, or a kid who has to stand in front of class to give a report. They know they've studied but they lock up, freeze, and panic.

Eddie Murphy is totally different offstage than onstage; he's quiet and doesn't act crazy at all. Each of us has to learn how to be that different person when we're "onstage."

Russell Simmons is the entertainment mogul whose initial record label, Def Jam, spawned many other businesses — Def Comedy Jam, production of the film *The Nutty Professor,* the clothing line Phat Farm, and the hip-hop Web site 360.com. He has, as well, grown and matured over the years. When he came to my agency, his name was always coming up in the gossip pages, and he wasn't taken seriously as a businessman. Initially, he was only interested in his work — not in being a public figure — so he was reluctant to do television interviews. He didn't like to present or accept awards and would only stand up and say, "Thank you." Over the years, he became more comfortable taking a stand on important issues, and he became much more vocal at public events. It was something that had to happen over a period of time.

Even comedian Chris Rock has said publicly on *60 Minutes* and other interviews that he's a master onstage, but in real life he's just a "scared little girl." It may surprise you, but this is the case with a lot of performers.

Michael Jackson is prolific onstage and moves millions of people, but in his social interactions he's very shy. Personal or private interactions are not easy for him.

Saskia Webber, a 1999 World Cup Soccer champion, used to be very shy, too. Saskia was backup to Briana Scurry, and she never thought she would have the chance to be on a championship team. She hung in there and ended up getting a lot of attention once the team started doing appearances.

"It is important to talk; a shy person can be helped to discover verbal skills, if you just talk to them. Talking lets others know what you think is important." — Helen

JOKING

Now, a certain amount of joking around is part of growing up, but be aware that if you go too far, someone could get hurt. And if you do hurt someone's feelings, don't be too proud to admit you were wrong and apologize.

It is *never, ever* acceptable to make fun of *anyone* for *any* reason. Not their hair, their clothes, their ethnic background, their religion, their economic status, their physical appearance, and especially not their mama. This is because of something I mentioned earlier. Remember that everything that goes around, comes around — and you never know where you will meet that person again years later.

GOSSIP

If you can't say anything good about somebody, don't say anything at all. If I'm asked about someone and I don't think the person is righteous, I try to make an effort to not speak unkindly. I might say, "There are things I have observed. But maybe there's another side to that person. You never know what's going on with people." Gossip isn't necessarily untrue. What you heard might be true — but it might not be the whole story.

You know what keeps me from gossiping? If you are going to dog somebody out, you put yourself in a position to be dogged out, too — plain and simple.

It doesn't make you feel good when you say unkind things about people. You could hurt someone's feelings or ruin someone's reputation — including your own when people know you were the source.

Sticks and Stones

Sticks and stones may break my bones / but words can never hurt me / Sticks and stones may break my bones/ but words can never ever hurt me / words can divert me / they can convert me from thinking my dreams can be real / words can divest me / and arrest me and all my ideas that percolate / ideas that generate / thoughts that I contemplate / and that define me. And refine me / and align me / with the person that I wanna to be / And I wanna see a reflection / that stands up to inspection / not a head that is wounded, and bleeding / conceding the dreams are no good / I've got to be stronger so I can last longer than the pain that the words have inflicted / and constricted and restricted / No I can't hide from the rain of destruction / But I can / keep my mind under construction / to fight with a

SLAMMIN' TRUTHS

sword / all the words with the truth / let it out of the booth to be free to compete / and defeat the words that somebody said can't hurt / make me feel like dirt, but I'm here to relay what they say can't / find a place in your head if you choose to be strong / if you choose to be strong / but I will not deny it's a lie that the words don't hurt cuz sometimes they do / but I will not deny its a lie that the words don't hurt cuz sometimes they do /
cuz sometimes they do /
cuz sometimes they do /
cuz sometimes they do

— Sharita Hunt

BREAKING CODES OF SILENCE

"When it comes to breaking silences, if you mean telling on someone, I don't want to be an informer. That could make it bad for me. When you inform, and when it gets found out that you are a snitch, it could be really bad." — Jason

"It might be right to tell if you know something bad about a kid, but that's just not me: I wouldn't tell. When you talk about a conscience, yeah, everybody has one, I guess. Sometimes my conscience makes me feel guilty, but I guess I ignore it. I don't always know the right thing to do. I guess a lot of kids are like me." — Melanie

The time will come for you to test your values, morals, and conscience, and whenever you do the right thing you *always, always* win. You've got to learn to perfect the skill of listening to your inner voice because it always tells you the right thing to do — even though you may have a tendency to ignore it, push it aside, and pretend you don't hear it. And when that governs you and you do the right thing, you always win.

How many violent acts could have been avoided if someone had decided to take a stand and speak up? Since the incident at Columbine High School in Littleton, Colorado, where fourteen people died in a shooting in August 1999, there has been a lot of discussion about school violence. That month's issue of *Teen People* focused on school violence around the country. The magazine interviewed all kinds of kids all over the country who told their stories about what happened on that day.

One of the kids *Teen People* spoke with was Fawn Williams, a twelve-year-old student from Port Huron, Michigan. She broke the "code of silence" when a friend told her that some boys in her class were planning to get a bunch of kids into the gymnasium and then kill them. After one sleepless night she went to the assistant principal and told what she knew. Ultimately, the boys were arrested and charged with conspiracy to commit murder. Fawn says, "To someone else in my situation, I'd say listen to your heart, think what's right. If people might get hurt, then the best thing to do is go forward. I know I'd do the same thing again."

Speaking up when you know something is wrong takes courage. You could be called a snitch or a tattletale. But I think saving lives is a fair trade-off with being called a name or two.

Fawn was afraid, but she knew she had done the right thing. Courage is not acting in the absence of fear, it's acting in the presence of fear. Imagine how many lives were probably saved because she spoke out.

No one may ever say a word to you, but you will be respected and admired for taking action. People notice what you do, but they don't always broadcast it.

I know school can be brutal. The teasing can get outrageous and the taunting sometimes violent. However, you must break the code of silence. Don't conceal information that could make a real difference for someone else. Report it anonymously if you have to, but report it.

"I think when a kid stands up for whatever they believe in, other people will respect them." — Marie

"All that is required for the triumph of evil is that good men remain silent and do nothing." — Edmund Burke, a famous philosopher

WHEN TALKING TURNS VIOLENT

Teasing among kids can be pretty merciless. Dr. Laurence Steinberg in *Teen People* has said that teens can exercise control of their school environment by "stepping in and reporting behavior that looks suspicious or potentially dangerous before there's a crisis, so that troubled kids can get help. 'Teenagers are the key to stopping this from happening, because they're the ones who often see the sides of a kid who might be dangerous,' says Steinberg. And while it can be impossible to spot a troubled teen from a class picture, there are warning signs, such as explosions of rage, lesser acts of violence in a kid's past, and written statements of violence."

High school is difficult for many people. Too many kids are picked on for things like having a low voice, being short, being smart, wearing unusual clothes — all kinds of things. Instead of getting to know someone, people make assumptions based on other people's appearance.

In response to the violence at Columbine, students across the country decided they had to take action. Rebecca Hunter in Nashville said, "The impression I got was that the students in the Trench Coat Mafia were made to feel like outcasts, and the violence comes from that." Some students, teachers, and parents from Rebecca's school composed the "I Will" pledge, which they printed on a petition and wallet-size cards for students to sign:

I Will Pledge

As part of my community and the ________ School District,

- **I will pledge to be part of the solution.**
- **I will eliminate taunting from my own behavior.**
- **I will encourage others to do the same.**
- **I will do my part to make my community a safe place by being more sensitive to others.**
- **I will set the example of a caring individual.**
- **I will eliminate profanity toward others from my language.**
- **I will not let my words or actions hurt others.**
- **. . . and if others won't become part of the solution, I WILL.**

People have always used violence to resolve conflict. But innocent people often get caught in the crossfire. The "I Will" pledge is a promise to be a part of the solution. When you are with a friend, boyfriend, or girlfriend, the minute — not the next few minutes, but *the minute* — he or she shows *any* violence toward you, end the relationship. End it the first time, before it escalates. I don't care how cute he is. I don't care how hot she is. If that person is violent toward you even a little bit, *get out* before it's too late. Get out before your self-esteem is totally shut down. Talk to someone about the incident, preferably your parents.

Danielle Fishel of the TV show *Boy Meets Girl,* describes an incident from her life in the book, *Got Issues Much?* by Randi Reisfeld and Marie Morreale. "We'd only been together for three weeks," she recalls. "It was a really new relationship. One day at school, I was talking to a good friend who happens to be a guy. I hadn't seen him for a few months, because he had graduated. He had come back for a visit. We were having a really great time talking, and all of a sudden my boyfriend came over, grabbed me by the arm, spun me around, and said, 'What are you doing?' "

" 'I'm talking to Matt,' I said. And he was like, 'You should not be over here talking. You're my girlfriend, and all my friends want to know what my girlfriend is doing talking to another guy.'

"He tried to drag me away, and I'm, like, 'Excuse me?!!!! You can tell your friends that if they have a problem they're not a part of our relationship. And if it's you who has the problem, you can turn around and say 'bye right now, but I want to talk to Matt.'

"So he did, and we broke up."

Right then and there Danielle knew that if she stopped talking to her friend Matt and followed her boyfriend over to his buddies, she would be in deep trouble. If she allowed it to happen once, Danielle knew it would happen again . . . and again . . . Danielle was aware that if she permitted him to get away with such bullish behavior, there was a chance that she could find herself in a seriously dangerous situation.

ISMS

I talked to my mom about isms. She's pretty wise. She said, "Isms are not about liking everybody, it's about respecting and understanding differences. It has more to do with your own culture and gender issues than the other person's race or sex or age."

A woman reporter publicly accused Charlie Ward, point guard for the New York Knicks, of being sexist because he doesn't think it is proper for anyone to be in the locker room when the guys are dressing and undressing — especially women. According to Charlie's Christian beliefs the only woman who should see a married man in the buff is his wife. But he remained firm in his conviction that he was being mis-portrayed. Charlie Ward is a deeply religious man. He always credits God for his success and ability. As a result, some people think of him as a zealot. Yet he has not wavered at all in his belief. He released a statement to express what he actually felt, and people eventually came to understand and respect his beliefs.

"Ism" thinking can be very unbalanced. It groups people into a category and robs them of their individuality. They — whoever "they" are — are not all the same. Every group has its good and bad individuals. Keep that in mind. Be careful when you start to think, "*They* always . . ." It's so easy to think *all* __________ (fill in the group or race of people) are dirty, have rhythm, can do math, have all the money. In school, you probably hear something like this a lot: "*They* (the cheerleaders, the drama group, the French club, the basketball team, the football team, the baseball team) think they're cute/macho. They get all the guys/girls . . ."

How often have we heard ourselves, friends, or family members say, "*We* [white people, black people,

Hispanic people, Asian people] are better because we are [white, black, Hispanic, Asian] and therefore should call all the shots."?

Isms can be very convenient excuses for the failures we experience in life. But we should never allow any kind of ism to get in the way of doing whatever we want to do. You can do anything you *want* to do, if you decide that you will not let anything get in your way.

An example of not bending to ageism is George Foreman. If he had thought he was too old, he would never have been heavyweight champion of the world at age forty-six.

Check your own behavior — comments, jokes, offhand remarks, and assumptions. And make sure you don't let "ism" thinking prevent you from being a success in life.

CONDOLENCES

"My best friend had lost her cousin in a terrible accident on a roller coaster at Coney Island. She was out of school several days because she was very upset. When she came back to school she asked me to just be there and be her friend. I helped her get through that tough time and it was satisfying to me to know that I helped somebody through a hard time." — Francisca

You almost have to go through a death or loss yourself to really appreciate how much a little card, note, or phone call can mean. When you buy and mail that card, it is hard to imagine that under the circumstances it will matter. But it does.

Your presence also means a lot. Not a bunch of words, but just your presence. At a funeral, when your friend steps out of the car and he or she sees you standing there, or when your friend walks down the aisle following the casket out and spots your face in the crowd, it helps. I know. *I've been there.* I can remember being pleasantly stunned but oh-so-touched by the presence of two colleagues who traveled a distance to attend my grandmother's funeral. I will never forget the feeling.

Sometimes people are so awkward and they say such weird things because they don't know what to say. I think the best thing is to say, "I am sorry for your loss . . . and is there any way I can help you?" Ask how they're doing and how other family members are doing. Say something special you remember about the person, or something that made you laugh. Maybe something you will most miss about the person. This allows them to share similar memories with you.

Sometimes people have a tendency to shy away from you when you have experienced a crisis. Family scandal, divorce — we don't know what to say or how to say it but we can send the person a note.

A lot of times people feel the need to express their condolences right after the person has experienced the hardship. In fact, six months from the date of the tragedy is the time you really can extend yourself. By that time, most people will have forgotten about it and don't think about saying anything. You can ask the person how they are doing on the anniversary of the death or tragedy. These are ways to really help uplift people. And again, they help you stand out.

"It is out of respect to send condolences to people who have lost loved ones. Little things mean a lot. I have a favorite teddy bear I send to people who are going through some things. I have about one hundred teddy bears. I love giving teddy bears. If someone I know is going through stuff, and I give them a get-well teddy bear, I feel great inside and I hope they feel better, too." — Brittany

In this fast-paced world, it's the little, the *littlest* things that will speak volumes. You can say or do something that will turn into a big thing. One small sweet sentence or gesture can brighten someone's day. I can tell you, it will cause people to go to the ends of the earth for you because you've touched them in a special way.

ON THE DOWN LOW

What you can say in a condolence card:

"I was sorry to hear about your loss. Please know that my thoughts and prayers are with you. And if you need a shoulder or friend, I'm here for you."

Talking helps you to understand other people better. Even in bad times and when you have prejudices. Just talking can save or change lives. So talk to new people. Set aside your slang and profanity, introduce yourself to someone who does not share your point of view. Venture into new territory with an open mind. Talk. How you talk is your business, and everyone else's with whom you talk.

"In school you gotta talk a certain way to teachers and stuff but with your friends you can talk the way you want to." — Nat

"If you are going to look for a job, you better not use that slang stuff, you know, 'phat,' 'dissing,' stuff like that. Just talk that way with your friends and when you don't want your parents to know what you are talking about." — Isaiah

"If I want someone to do something, I better talk in a way they can understand. Also when I am talking in class, if I don't want to be embarrassed, I need to think about how I am talking." — Tiffany

"If I want to ask a girl out she better know what I am saying." — Brandon

"I wish you would talk to my dad about this. He thinks he can talk to me in any way because I am his kid. He just doesn't get it and he makes me so mad." — Jon

"But you know what? The way you talk reflects the kind of person you are, like people might think you are from the ghetto if you don't speak well." — Tracy

"My mom told me — and I don't always do everything she says, but this one is good — she said people judge who you are by how you dress and talk. She said that if you want to get ahead you better dress and talk like people in business. I guess maybe then if that is true, how I talk might be everybody's business." — Tamela

"A kid in my class has bad manners. He ruins it for everybody else." — Luis

"People know good manners. They just don't show them. It's not cool sometimes, especially with your friends." — Brandi

"I am really different with my friends than with my parents. I don't really care with my friends." — Will

I have a "little sister" named Tamicka, who is sixteen years old and is in high school in New York City. Tamicka and I spend a lot of time together — she comes to my office and helps out, we have a fun time together. We talk a lot about school and all kinds of things. Tamicka once told me that her school principal had done some special things for her and gone out of her way to help her. So I asked Tamicka if she had ever taken the time to thank her principal. And you know what? She hadn't thought about it.

So I suggested to Tamicka that she find out the

date of her principal's birthday. It was coming up soon, so Tamicka and I picked out a beautiful birthday card. Tamicka wrote a special thank-you and happy birthday message and left the card on the principal's desk. The principal was so touched and blown away by Tamicka's simple gesture that she invited her to go on a special weekend field trip that she had not been slated to attend. Tamicka was one of a few selected students who were invited.

When you acknowledge someone for his or her time and thoughtfulness, it makes that person feel special. Often they are willing to do special things for you!

The truth of the matter is that people tend to be wrapped up in their own day-to-day needs. So simple things like a thank-you note or phone call can get lost. An actor friend sent a thank-you note to the director and playwright after an audition. When she saw them several days later, the director commented on the fact that it had been a long time since anyone had sent her a thank-you note. People don't do it. It's so rare that when it happens, you stand out — in a major way.

What's uncool about "please" and "thank you"? What's uncool about "excuse me"? Some people think manners are useless, phony, or depend on the setting.

But you never know who's paying attention, who's watching you from a distance, who's right there in your face, impressed by the way you treat others with respect.

REAL STORIES

Tamika and Douglas

"Tamika, Douglas," Mom called. "Have you guys finished those thank-you notes yet? I'm leaving here in five minutes and I can drop them in the mailbox on the corner."

Douglas and I are twins. Fraternal. We look nothing alike. Anyway, our birthday was last week. We turned fifteen. We got some great stuff from Mom and Dad — clothes and stuff like that. And our grandparents gave us each fifty bucks. Our older brother, Dennis, who we think looks like Denzel, upgraded our computer. Well, we thanked them all. We called Grandpa and Grandma right away, and I gave "Denz" the biggest hug. There is so much more we can do now, and that computer just flies, it's so fast.

And then there's my father's sister, Aunt Clarise, who sent us both these really weird gifts.

I guess Aunt Clarise means well, but . . . bookends? Bookends. I would have gotten a gift certificate for a CD or a video.

The bookends Aunt Clarise gave me look like something Xena the Warrior Princess would use to conquer an enemy. At least *mine* looked like medieval weaponry or something you could give a name to. What Dougie got was even stranger. The bookends were like two twisted blobs. Like something she made in art class. If my friends came in my room and saw those things they'd laugh me out of the neighborhood. We are supposed to be thankful?

Since our birthday was last week, Mom says we can't wait anymore. She says it's rude if we don't do it soon.

But why do we have to lie to Aunt Clarise? I wish we could just forget about it!

THANK YOU

An expression of gratitude makes the other person feel good. You may not have gotten exactly what you wanted — but you need to let Aunt Clarise know you appreciate that she thought of you. The weird bookends might be useful someday, but more important, Tamika and Douglas have an aunt who cares about them.

I know someone who gave a present to a couple because she really liked them. They had said thank you at the time. But then thirty years later, she went to visit the couple unannounced. There in the hall, in full view, hung the picture she had given them. She was transformed and felt so special that after all the time that had passed, the gift was still a part of their lives.

The day will come when you get a gift you just don't like. You still express your gratitude. I recommend you focus on the gesture. I've gotten many a gift I didn't like . . . so I share the goodies.

Let me give you another example of what a simple "thank you" can do.

My agency was fortunate enough to work with filmmaker Matty Rich in 1992. This very talented young man wrote, produced, directed, and starred in the critically acclaimed film *Straight Out of Brooklyn* — at age nineteen! Bill Reel, a columnist for *New York Newsday,* devoted an entire column — unsolicited — to the importance of Matty and his stunning debut film. I mentioned to Matty that it would really be nice to acknowledge this effort and suggested we send a thank-you note on a *Straight Out of Brooklyn* postcard. The result: This very busy columnist, who rarely takes time out for lunch, let alone press conferences, came to a press conference set up to announce Matty's latest project. Bill said he'd come just to meet Matty because of that thank-you note. Not that he expects them, Bill said, but in his fifteen years in business he had received only three thank-you notes for columns — and Matty's was one of them.

REAL STORIES

Dear Douglas and Tamika

Dear Douglas and Tamika,
I was so happy to hear you received the bookends. I sent them because I wanted you to know how much I think of you and want you to succeed in school and in life. Tamtam, when I saw the bookends that looked like the sword and the spiky ball, I thought

REAL STORIES

of you because you are a fighter — I can see you holding your own and taking good care of yourself. Dougie, I made the bookends for you in my ceramics class. Do you remember the time you gave me an ashtray you made in art class? I wasn't sure what it was, but it came in handy anyway. I want to encourage you to continue with your art.

Your father tells me you both like music. In the paper I read that a new music and video superstore is opening in your town. You should be receiving two $50 gift certificates in the mail in about a week. I hope you don't mind shopping for your own goodies — I can't keep up with your tastes. Enjoy!

Love,
Aunt Clarise

ON THE DOWN-LOW

Spelling People's Names Correctly

Spelling people's names correctly is also a sign of respect. It's a little thing but it's super-important.

I often receive correspondence that begins with "Dear Teri" or "Terri" or "Terry." There have even been a few addressed to *Mr.* Terry Williams! This is an immediate turnoff — it shows that the writer didn't care enough to check out the spelling of my name or even my gender!

One of my first mentors, Ken Smikle, made up notecards for me that have the three wrong spellings of my name on the front with lines crossed through them. On the inside it says: "From T-E-R-R-I-E . . . Thanks." Great idea! I send a notecard to people when they repeatedly spell my name wrong, and it never fails to get my point across.

Entertainment Weekly magazine took the NBC network and Warner Bros. to task for this particular kind of slipup. It seems an ad produced by NBC misspelled megadirector Steven Spielberg's name. And then Warner Bros. made a mistake in a press release that announced a film deal with *Jurassic Park* author Michael Crichton.

You always want to spell people's names correctly. It's a sign of being thorough — especially if the person's name is usually misspelled.

If you make a mistake, just be certain to acknowledge or apologize for it.

Being mannerly — acting with respect — needs to be the order of the day. However, no one is perfect. People often act selfishly and forget their manners altogether. We need to learn to think about *what* we're doing, and *where* we're doing it.

I gave someone a compliment one time and instead of saying thank you, she said, 'I know. You don't have to tell me.' That proves her parents didn't teach her manners." — Omar

For instance, sometimes people will respond to you rudely, for no reason at all. But their words should not be taken personally. Sometimes people are walking around with emotional baggage, and they are reacting today because of some problem they've been carrying around for years. It's important to keep that in mind. We don't always see what happened to that person before we met them. Give the person the benefit of the doubt. And if you're really bugged by the incident, talk with a friend, go ahead and whine some, and then concentrate more on letting it go than letting it fester.

MANNERS AT HOME

At home, familiarity makes us forget to be considerate; and it is very easy to get on one another's nerves. The telephone can be a major source of conflict. But it doesn't have to be.

REAL STORIES

Beep, Beep, Click, Click

Tiffany and Amy are best friends. They talk to each other on the phone every day after school. A lot can happen between 3 P.M. and 5 P.M. They need to know everything. As far as Tiffany and Amy are concerned everything is a late-breaking news flash to be reported instantly and at great length. That's what's so good about call waiting.

Tiffany painted her fingernails a shocking cobalt blue while she and Amy were catching up. "So Amy, Tony, like, just walked up to Angie and started talking to her. He is, like, so fine."

Suddenly, there was the insistent call waiting, beep, beep. "Hold on, Amy, be right back." Click. "Hello. Hi, Mr. Richards. Okay, got it. Soccer practice canceled today. I'll tell my mom. Bye." Click.

"Hi, Amy, so tell me, Angie actually, like, spoke to Tony?" Beep, beep. "Is that yours? Okay, I'll hold." Tiffany could hardly contain herself. Angela and Tony. They would make a hot couple.

Mom came into the room. Tiffany still thought her mom's new glasses were ugly. A lot of good they did — Mom still lost track of her car keys. "Tiffany, I need to make a call before I take your sister to soccer practice. Have you seen my car keys?"

"No, and soccer practice has been canceled. Mr. Richards just called."

Click.

"That was Angie? You just talked to Angie? No, he didn't. You mean like a date?" Tiffany looked up and her mom was just standing there. "Hold on, Ame. Wait a minute."

Tiffany's mom stood looking at her. Tiffany could tell her mom was starting to get angry.

"Mom," Tiffany said, "as soon as I get all the rest of the details, I promise I'll get off."

"No, Tiffany. You can call Amy back. I've been patient but now I need to use the phone. Tiff, you're not the only who lives here."

"I'll have to call you back," Tiffany said grudgingly. Tiffany thought her mom's tone was snotty. "Just wait till I get my own phone," Tiffany said under her breath.

ON THE DOWN-LOW

Table Manners

Here are just a few hints from Ms. Demeanor:

- Sit up straight. You'll actually be more comfortable.
- Don't talk with your mouth full. Take small bites. Finish chewing.
- Break the bread and butter one piece at a time.
- Don't leave lipstick stains on glasses or cups.
- Be careful not to eat too fast. When eating with others, everyone should start and finish each course about the same time.
- Spread the napkin across your lap and leave it there. If you leave the table temporarily, leave the napkin on your chair and slide the chair under the table. The napkin

should be used to carefully dab the corners of your mouth.

- Purses, briefcases, keys, hats, gloves – anything that is not part of the meal – do not belong on the table. It is unsightly and unsanitary.

If all else fails, remember that courtesy, kindness, and common sense can get you through most dining experiences.

MANNERS AT SCHOOL

Using manners or being considerate means putting aside our own immediate gratification to accommodate others. It is also about how you, in turn, expect or want to be treated. The same principle applies to school.

School is a place where you learn life and social skills, make friends, and have a good time. There are lots of rules to maintain order and to make sure that the environment is conducive to learning. After all, the main point of school is to get an education and absorb information that will help you later. School rules ensure that education can take place in school. But so do manners.

Using manners makes a difference in how and what you learn in school.

REAL STORIES

Just Beep Me

This whole thing was whack! Raul had just forgotten to the turn the beeper off. As far as he was concerned having a beeper was all right. He wasn't trying to make a drug connection. He was only interested in the love connection.

Most of the time Mr. Davidson was cool, but today with the beeper thing, he was just out of control. He didn't understand. Raul had to be in touch. He had to be reachable. When Rosanna said she would tell him when she was free, he was very glad. Rosanna was da bomb. She looked good in jeans, got good grades, and had hair down to here. The fact that she went to the prep school across town didn't hurt, either.

They had met at the mall one Thursday afternoon. It was at the Gap where she had a part-time job. Her smile lit up the whole store. And eyes. The girl had eyes. He had to be reachable when she called. And now this — *a write-up and a warning.*

If it was turned off what was the big deal? It wasn't like you couldn't pay attention in class. Like geology was so interesting. What *was* the problem?!

Think about it: Can you really concentrate if, in the back of your mind, you are expecting to be beeped or pulsed at any given moment? It is a sign of respect for your teachers and fellow students when beepers and cell phones are not allowed to ring. If there is a "no beeper/cell phone" rule in your school, observe it. Your school has a system in place to reach you when there is a real emergency.

MANNERS IN THE WORLD

"Bad manners make you look like you weren't raised right." — Jennifer

When you behave in a mannerly fashion it shows respect for those around you. When people feel respected, they feel good. And when you show respect for others, it demonstrates that you have respect for yourself, too.

Manners and Sense Rap

Speakin' of manners / speakin' of sense / brothers and sisters don't sit on the fence / Boogers outch your nose / like a smellin' in your shoe / like passsssin' gassss won't do / all your manners at a loss / pickin' your nose in front of us is gross / for your manners prescription you need a dose / shows your manners quotient is way, way low / risin' in the ranks is gonna be slow / if you can't even give your nose a good blow / man, you gotta keep your nose clean / how you ever gonna make the sho nuf scene / showin' you lacking somethin' in your hygiene / put your manners in gear / 'cause this posse you're with here is down with manners / we carry our pride like banners / that wave / that say we're cool / in the cream-of-crop pool!

— Sharita Hunt

My mother said if you get used to a bad habit and just let it go, you could really be embarrassed. True story. I have a habit of belching. After my mother's warning, I became more cautious. But one night I was walking down the street when I felt a belch coming on. I didn't see anyone so I let it out. A man in a car I had not seen described me in language even I can't repeat. (Well, you know I can but I won't.) My mother's words could not have been proven more true than that night on a "deserted" street.

Manners are a must when the setting is more formal, but that does not mean you totally let it go the rest of time. And you don't have to wait until you're in a formal situation, like a wedding, to show your best side.

REAL STORIES

Monique

Monique remembered being ecstatic when her cousin Lauren had asked her to be a bridesmaid. Lauren was her favorite cousin. She was cool. A good dresser. She had a great job and knew a lot of important people. Some of those celebrities would surely come to the wedding. And there Monique would be, in the middle of it all.

Lauren had picked out some fabulous dresses. Of course, Monique just knew the dress was going to look better on her than the other bridesmaids. Her hair appointment was made for early tomorrow morning. Monique knew she was going to look *gooood!*

Lauren had given her a special hug last night when they finished making the decorations. She knew she was Lauren's favorite.

Well, they lined up the bridesmaids and the groomsmen according to height. And wouldn't you know it, the tallest and ugliest boy was Monique's escort. How could Lauren do that to her? She was going to be recorded for all time in pictures with the ugliest boy in the world.

There must be a way to change this around. When Monique asked the wedding coordinator about changing the lineup, all the woman said was, "You'll have to talk to the bride about that."

Sometimes you just don't know what the mannerly course of action is. One way to avoid being embarrassed or hurting others is to ask an adult you trust what is appropriate and what is not. Monique's self-centered attitude is not cool. Sometimes things happen and they are not the way you would choose. And there is only one thing to do — be gracious and be supportive. A responsible, loving adult would advise Monique to chill, get with the program. "It's not your day. It's their day. It's about the bride and the groom."

ON THE DOWN-LOW

Public Transportation

When you and your friends use it, remember you're sharing it with the rest of the world. It is good manners to be mindful of those around you. One way of doing that is to keep your conversation to a low roar. If you must make or receive a call on your cell phone, try to keep the tone of your voice down and the conversation brief. Your business is just that — *your* business. Be careful of your language. Even if the people around you are strangers, you can still show them some respect. See what a difference it can make when you use a little self-control.

KEEPING YOUR WORD

Ever heard anyone say, "Let your yes be yes and your no, no"? Or "your word is your bond"?

Deborah Hayes, who was Oprah Winfrey's vice president of corporate communications for five years, said that in all the time she worked with her, Oprah never canceled or postponed an interview or photo session. She treated people with respect and courtesy. Susan Taylor, former publication director for *Essence* magazine, mentioned that whenever Oprah agreed to be on a cover or participate as host of an *Essence* Awards show, she was always gracious and punctual. It can be a rare thing, especially for such a powerful person.

REAL STORIES

Asha and Meghan

Monday

Asha and Meghan usually met at about 11:45 outside the cafeteria. Meghan remembered how when Asha first showed up at school she really stood out. And that they immediately liked each other. Asha was very easy to talk to, and she had a lot of interesting stories about her family and their trips to India. Meghan had introduced Asha around to some of the other kids.

Asha came running up. "Sorry I'm late. Ms. Stevens kept me. I have to rewrite my English paper. But that's not important." When Asha got excited she talked really fast and nonstop. "My aunt Sujatha and uncle Anand are coming to America this week, and we are having a big party for them on Friday night and I want you to come. Can you?"

"Is your mom going to make those little pies with the potato filling?"

"Samosas? Sure. So you'll come?"

"Yeah! It sounds really nice."

"Oh, good. Let's eat."

Wednesday

The tryouts for the cheerleading team were Wednesday afternoon. Asha sat in the bleachers and watched as Meghan finished her combination with a flawless split. Asha could tell that the captains of the cheerleading team, Sean and Wendy, were really impressed. They should have been. Meghan was great!

Thursday

The names for the new cheerleading squad were posted. Of course, Meghan made the team and was flying. Making the cheerleading squad was an important achievement. Their high school was known for their cheerleading squad and had won all kinds of trophies and ribbons. Asha bought Meghan's dessert at lunch that day as a way of saying, "Congratulations!"

Friday

Meghan was hanging her jacket in her locker when she heard her name. It was Sean and Wendy, the captains of the cheerleading squad.

Sean said, "All of us on the cheerleading squad are going out to the Grill tonight."

"We want you to come," Wendy added.

"Yeah, sure!" Meghan said, trying to be cool. Then she remembered Asha. "No, wait." She paused for a moment then said, "Yeah, sure."

"All right," Sean said. "Seven o'clock. See you at the Grill."

Meghan figured Asha would understand.

You know what Meghan is doing, don't you? She's saying Asha isn't as important as the cheerleading squad. But if you promise to do something with a friend, it is your responsibility to follow through. Keeping your word is always the right thing to do and it's a good character trait.

There may have been a way for Meghan to gracefully get out of going to Asha's party after having made a commitment four days earlier. But not showing up is just rude! Things happen. We all understand that and make allowances — if we're shown the courtesy of an explanation in advance.

Manners give us guidelines to live respectfully with one another. Courteous behavior starts at home and extends to the rest of the world. You did not get to choose the group of people known as your family. They can be hard to get along with at times. But you have to live with them. Being considerate of one another — how much time you spend on the phone, in the bathroom, resisting the temptation to borrow that fly new sweater that belongs to your sister or brother — can go a long way toward keeping the peace.

You spend a lot of time at school. There, you can

choose the people you hang out with. Treat the members of your posse with respect. Be sensitive to their feelings.

When you have a working knowledge of manners and use them, you contribute to everyone's well-being. Even strangers. We are always in contact with them, especially in public places like movie theaters. And considering the price of a movie ticket, you want to sit comfortably, hear every word, see every gesture and not be distracted by those who think they are at home in their own living rooms.

Manners begin and end with you. Even if no one else uses them, you'll benefit from showing respect.

"People should act in a certain way, you know, civil to each other." — Amy

"Being mannerable doesn't really suck." — Eric

"Manners are rules, not just rules, common courtesy. It's about being nice." — Mary

"Manners are important. That's how I was raised." — Omar

"I think that's the only way some kids know how to be. They learn it from their parents. They learn it from their peers. This is the only way they know how to be — sexually, with money or anything. When they say I am getting mine, that is all they know how to do really. That is the way they cope. Kids don't know any other way. They have been taught to get things for themselves and they will do what they feel will get them what they want." — Brittany

"I think people who say, 'I'm getting mine. It's all about me' are really selfish. But in this world I guess it is how you gotta be." — Amy

You can choose to go through this world all by yourself. Your motto could be solely looking out for number one. But I encourage you to figure other people into the equation of a successful life. You do have to look out for yourself, but we all need people to support us and help us in our lives. As I talk with you on these pages, I'm talking to myself, too.

GETTING YOURS

There are lots of ways to win, to get what you want in this world. You can step on everyone along the way, be ruthless and thoughtless. You can be as smart and shrewd as you can be. You can press forward refusing to take no for an answer or defeat as an outcome.

But now say it with me: Everything that goes around comes around.

When you step over or on top of people, it comes back to you. To get yours at any cost can mean a lot of loneliness in the future. You do yourself a grave disservice if you must win at all costs every time you attempt something. Your goal can't be to do better than someone else. Instead, compare yourself to who you were six months ago, a year ago. You will be stronger if your goal is to do and be the best you can. As you struggle toward that goal, you won't always be the winner. But if you learn from your losses, your ability to win will become stronger. And when you do win, you will appreciate the prize because you know what it took to get it.

Dave Winfield, a New York Yankees All-Star, was always honorable and reputable. But he began to be maligned by the team owner, George Steinbrenner. Steinbrenner's public relations team planted negative items about Dave because Steinbrenner didn't want to continue to pay him. Some people questioned Dave but he always held his head high. Years later, after Dave left and retired, Steinbrenner reached out to him, apologized, and asked him to come to a game. Finally they made peace.

REAL STORIES

Sportsmanlike Conduct

The last thing Henry, the captain of the team, remembered as they lined up for the next down was saying to the captain of the opposing team, a rich dude named Tyler, "You did that on purpose. You guys are gonna pay."

Before the captain, who played center, could say anything, one of the guards said, "Try it, you big —"

And Henry was on him like white on rice. His objective in life became to hurt as many members of the opposing team as he could. He grabbed the guard's face mask with full intent to break his neck. Henry, who was a nose tackle, was very big and powerful.

"All right, you guys break it up. Break it up I said." It was the coach — and Henry recognized another voice as his dad's. The referees, coaches, and some parents came down onto the field to break up the fight. It was the worst fight the team had been in. Henry had been aware of the sound of bodies in combat, their helmets crashing against one other and the ground. He connected with a couple good punches. Security guards came down into the stadium bleachers in case the spectators tried to get into the fray. One guy from the other team had gotten hit so hard in the groin he was crying.

The coach took Henry out of the game and fined him for starting the fight, but Henry didn't care. The opposing team had intentionally targeted Derrick, the quarterback, to make sure he was out of the game. Henry couldn't let that go.

Henry sat on the bench for the rest of the game. He didn't care. He just wanted these rich punks to know they could not get away with what they'd done. Henry wasn't having it. His team lost the game but Henry didn't care. All he wanted to do was go to the hospital and see Derrick.

Henry, the coach, and a couple of Derrick's good friends went to the hospital right after the game. The doctor said that even though Derrick's leg was broken, he would probably be able to play again next season. Henry was relieved that Derrick was going to be okay. Henry went to Derrick's mother and said, "I'm sorry."

She shook his hand and said, "I am, too. Thanks for coming down. It means a lot to Derrick that you guys came."

Henry moved away really quickly, 'cause he could feel the tears coming up and if they started . . . well, he didn't even want to think about it.

The coach tried to talk him into going to meet the rest of the team for pizza and burgers.

"Hey, Hank, you're the captain. You gotta be there." But Henry didn't want to. He rode his motorcycle to the Friendly's where he knew his parents, little sister Amy, and her best friend Lisa would be. By the time he got there they were looking at the menus for dessert.

"How's Derrick doing?" his mother asked.

"He'll be okay," Henry replied.

"Glad to hear it, son," his father said. "We know why you did what you did, but you messed up. You lost your cool. You'll never win like that."

"It was just such a shame what happened to Derrick," his mother said.

"Those creeps were way too rough," Lisa said. "You could tell it was deliberate. They wanted him out of the game."

"Will he walk again?" his gloom-and-doom little sister asked.

"Sure he will, dummy, it's a broken leg," Henry snapped.

"Just 'cause they kicked you out of the game, doesn't mean you have to call names," Amy replied. "Idiot," she said under her breath.

"Twerp," he said under his breath.

Brother and sister glared at each other. Amy kicked his shin under the table. "Ow," Henry yelped.

"All right, you two," Dad intervened.

Henry looked up and saw Tyler Davidson, the captain of the winning team, coming in with his parents and some friends. He was surprised to see that Tyler wasn't out celebrating the championship at some fancy restaurant with the rest of the team. The waiters had to move some tables to accommodate them all. As Tyler glanced around the room, he and Henry made eye contact.

Henry felt anger rising up again. He was about to stand up when he realized Lisa was holding his hand so tight it hurt. The next thing he knew Tyler was walking over to their table.

"Hey, Henry," he said.

"You're Tyler Davidson," Henry's father said.

"My team screwed up bad tonight," Tyler said to Henry. "Real bad, and I just want to say, captain to captain, I don't blame you, I'd have done the same thing. I'm sorry. Is Derrick gonna be okay?"

"Yeah," Henry said.

The two looked at each other for an awkward moment and then Tyler said, "Well, see ya," and went to rejoin his family.

Henry and his family watched them all and for a moment the group glanced over at them. Then Henry saw Tyler's father put his arm around his son as they went to their table.

The winning team's coach had been a pro ballplayer, they had great new uniforms, and their school provided them with the best practice equipment. But apparently all that did not make them good sportsmen. Henry grinned to himself and thought, *They were scared of us and that's what they had to do to stop us.*

"What?" his family and Lisa said in unison.

"Nothin'," he said.

Now he really was hungry. So, he ordered a double cheeseburger with fries and a large Coke and a hot-fudge sundae for dessert.

The rich team seemed to have everything it needed to be winners. But they lacked confidence in their ability and resorted to brutality just to win the game. Henry lost control when he led the members of his team to use violence to get back at the other team. Just because somebody appears on the surface to be doing well doesn't mean that is the case. The very thing that you envy in somebody else could be masking pain or insecurity.

It is normal sometimes to be jealous or to want something someone else has. We all do it. It's something I battle with every day. I have to make a conscious effort to remind myself that no matter what it looks like, I have no idea what price a person might have to pay to keep up that image. I remind myself that I, too, have things that others may envy. We're all blessed in different ways.

Author Veronica Chambers said in *O* magazine, "Jealousy can tell you powerful things — what you want, what you must work harder to get, and what you have to let go. If you examine why you are jealous, the process will show you what your secret desires are. And you can use that knowledge to become the person you want to be."

So how do you get yours? What is a winning formula? The equation might look something like this.

$$NQ(P) + G + F^4 + G^2 + EXL(too) = R^3 + S$$

Of course, this isn't a real mathematical formula or equation but it was fun coming up with it. It breaks down like this:

NQ (not quitting) *P* (perseverance) means you have dreams and desires in life that you simply cannot give up on. Your gifts and talents need to be developed and may require a lot of hard work to become excellent. But I promise you if you hang in there, you won't be sorry.

Star Jones, who came to the public's attention when she was a commentator for *The Today Show* and is now one of the costars of the show *The View*, struggled most of her life with weight issues. Finally, through her mother's encouragement and support, she came to accept her size. She started developing a healthy attitude about it, wrote a book, and became quite the fashion plate. Star cultivated a real following for herself and is now considered a diva role model for plus-size women.

Natalie Cole struggled with drug abuse over the years and had trouble defining herself as a musician. She persevered and struggled. Eventually, through the magic of technology, she sang a duet with her famous father, the late Nat King Cole. The song, "Unforgettable," ended up winning several Grammys.

Get encouragement from those who went before you.

G means giving in ways that help others. Even if it's noticing first that the trash needs to be taken out and doing it for your mom or washing the car for your dad. Helping out around the house may not seem like much but your contribution to the household lets your parents know that you don't take your place in the world for granted.

F means failing a lot of times as you pursue your dreams. It means not being defeated. You must experience the valleys. When you reach the mountaintop you'll understand, and you'll appreciate what it took to get there.

Reverend Al Sharpton, the crusader for social justice, was stabbed in Bensonhurst, New York, and went to visit his assailant in jail. This visit allowed Sharpton to forgive, and now he corresponds with the attacker.

Malik Yoba was shot when he was in his teens. He went on to lecture and talk about gang violence and gun control. You need to turn lemons into lemonade.

Johnnie Cochran's brother was murdered, and yet he continues to fight for criminal justice.

Susan Taylor was a single mother who had no formal education but took her life into her hands and overcame her obstacles, rising to the top of *Essence* magazine. (Later she went on to obtain college and graduate school degrees.) Each of these people had valleys, but they didn't *stay* in the valley.

G^2 means giving more — doing some volunteer work such as baby-sitting for a single mother so she can run some necessary errands, or being a big brother or sister to a younger child.

EXL(too) means expressions of love and thinking

of others. Send friends and family a note or an e-mail, or give that annoying sibling a hug. Random acts of kindness go a long way to make the people who matter most to you feel really good.

$R^3 + S$ means receiving real rewards and success. All of the above equals having yours — your dream or goal, genuine friendships that last a lifetime, and unknown benefits from what you've done to make the world better. You may not even know how you have influenced someone along the way, but you will be remembered for your contribution to his or her life. And in actualizing your goals and dreams, you will experience success in life. Remember:

$$NQ(P) + G + F^4 + G^2 + EXL(too) = R^3 + S$$

RELATIONSHIPS

You can get yours and it can be all about you, but don't count on having any relationships of substance. The root word is "relate." To connect, to link, are synonyms for "relate" — and it's impossible to do these things if you're totally focused on yourself.

Relationships are give and take. We don't receive

if we don't give. Relationships can resemble a potluck dinner. It is rude to come to the table if you don't bring a dish. Takers let others do for them. They take advantage. They are the ones who get called and never call. They hog the conversation and rarely listen to others.

On the other hand there are the people who give to their families, friends, and communities. Whatever contributions they make, people find a way to acknowledge and thank them. The appreciation can be anything from a hug or an engraved plaque to an original song.

That's what Shaquille O'Neal of the Los Angeles Lakers did. He wrote a song about the man who was most important in his life — his stepfather, the man who raised him. It's hard enough to raise, care for, and be responsible for your own flesh-and-blood kids. But he was there for Shaq even though he was not his own blood. I admire people who are willing to adopt older children, take in foster kids, and provide love and care for kids who are suffering. People like Mother Hale and her daughter Lorraine, who started Hale House to care for children who were born with AIDS. When I see and hear about men and women giving of themselves, I am encouraged because I know those investments will pay off.

Guard your friendships. It is very easy to take friends for granted. There will always be times when one will call more often than the other does. But beware of one-sidedness. We sometimes expect our friends to read our minds and get with our program or vice versa. Be sure to express your thoughts.

Friendships last when people invest time in one another. The dynamic will change from time to time, but a relationship of caring people will endure all kinds of changes. I have a friend who went to therapy for a while when she realized that she seemed to be behaving badly toward one particular friend. She wasn't crazy, just depressed, but she also made it a personal policy to make sure she was more considerate of her friend. She said, "I don't have many friends, and I can't screw up with the ones I do have."

If you move through life totally focused on yourself, your life will not matter to anyone when you're gone. What you put out comes back to you. You have to give to get. You gain dividends on money you invest. But in order to get the dividend you have to take the money out of your pocket. You risk losing a great deal if the market goes down. Likewise, a moment of insensitivity or jealousy can put a perfectly solid relationship at risk. It takes work to maintain a healthy relationship. Part of that work is building a foundation of trust, caring, and respect. It is a lot easier to forgive someone for insensitivity if it is not an ongoing pattern. People move in and out of our lives all the time. What are the little things you can do to not mess up a relationship just because you're not in one person's company all the time? How do we prevent "out of sight, out of mind"?

STAYING IN TOUCH

A lot of times, "out of sight" becomes "out of mind" because we get caught up in our day-to-day activities, responsibilities, and challenges. I don't believe people adopt that attitude on purpose. We get overwhelmed, or we procrastinate and the time slips away. Staying in touch is hard — but if we do it, we stand out.

Staying in touch has probably been one of *the* hallmarks of my success. Staying in touch has made a huge difference in my business. I will admit it's probably a little easier for me because I enjoy people. I think I have been given a gift of being able to feel deeply what people are going through.

If someone has touched my life, I want the

person to know how much they mean to me. I might drop them a note from time to time, send a postcard to say hello, or send an article I think would interest them.

It is interesting that my little notes or articles often prompt a person to think about me for tickets to something, or give me information that will help me with my work. I have had many amazing things happen because I've stayed in touch with people. But my interest in people is not only for how they can help my success. (I've had far too many people care about me to even entertain that attitude.) As much as I care and as people-oriented as I am naturally, it is still an act of will, a decision to stay in touch.

It's no problem being in touch when folks are in your face. And it's no problem to lose touch when they're not. Life happens and there are all kinds of circumstances that separate us. Your best friend moves away when one of his parents gets a new job and the family has to relocate. Because of death or divorce or even legal action, your mall buddy has to go to another place to live.

Every year George Clooney, film actor and former *ER* star, rents a bus with eight of his old college buddies. They take a tour and go fishing. He says the purpose of this is to keep grounded. Your true friends know about your "dirt." Keeping in touch with real friends prevents us from believing our own hype.

During my five years at *Essence* magazine, I constantly stayed in touch with people. Whenever I came across an article I thought would be of interest to someone *Essence* had worked with, I would send it. When I left *Essence* and started my business, many of those people became my clients. I met celebrities such as Anita Baker and Janet Jackson while working at *Essence.* If you are in regular touch, people will remember you.

Charles Smith, a former player for the New York Knicks and San Antonio Spurs, would always call people in the cities in which he was playing, just to touch base and say hello. Since he did that over the ten years he played and during his tenure as a representative with the player's union, he was able to launch a new media technology company based on the relationships that he established when he was playing.

You can have good intentions to maintain contact when your friend moves away or goes to a different school, but then you get caught up in other things. After a certain amount of time has gone by, it's embarrassing to call or write. Remember, it's *never* too late to reach out. You can do it with a cute card, a simple gift, an interesting clipping, even an e-mail or voice-mail message. Of course, phone calls are the next-best thing to being there.

A letter doesn't have to be a long drawn-out thing. A postcard and a short message can make your friend laugh. Remember what you felt like when someone let you know they were thinking of you.

REAL STORIES

Dear Kellie,

Brian brought the card home from school today. He remembers you from English class last year. He says that one of the cheerleaders you stay in contact with wrote you about our family tragedy. Even though it has been six months, losing Linda and Mickie so early in their young lives continues to be a shock to our family. Linda was so excited about getting her driver's license. Brian misses his big sister and baby brother, and Ken and I miss our children. I am so glad that Brian has classmates who can express sup-

port, even if they have moved away. I want to thank you for your kindness. It was very thoughtful of you. Your card came at a time when I was personally very low and it helped me. Thank you again.
Dana, Ken, and Brian Morrisey

Dealing with all kinds of public personalities in my public relations business, I see that as long as the star is on top, they have friends everywhere. But as soon as the fame and prestige are gone, so are many of the friends and relationships. It's pathetic. I've said this before, and I'll say it again, treat people the way you want to be treated. You'll have friends for a lifetime.

"Talking about romantic relationships — guys like it when females treat them like garbage. When you are nice they run all over you and treat you mean. So I decided if that is what they want — to be treated like garbage — then I will do it." — Maya

Allowing someone else's negative actions to change the core of who you are gives someone else control over your life. It means that you will never stand for anything until you change.

Ask yourself, "Is it worth it to behave in a mean-spirited and careless way just to be able to say I have a girlfriend or boyfriend?" If the roles were reversed, how would you want to be treated? If you are nice to a person and they treat you like garbage, why would you continue to stay with that person for any longer than a minute? If we can't appreciate one another and be kind to one another, then what's the point? Remember, what goes around comes around.

It concerns me that some of you may be forming "serious" relationships before you are emotionally mature enough to handle them — or starting relationships without enough information. "Coming-of-age" television shows may be directed toward you, but remember the scripts are written by people who manipulate the outcome. Their job is to create drama, not always to represent real life.

GO OUTSIDE YOUR COMFORT ZONE

One of the major keys for success is being observant and responding to human needs. The environments we live and work in can be overwhelming and you might want to shut out everything around you, to take in only what's easy. But there can be a lot of satisfaction and positive stimulation when you reach out. It may be something as simple as offering to hold a cup of coffee for someone who is struggling to find their bus fare while juggling a briefcase and paper bag with a doughnut.

Reach out and help someone. It's absolutely amazing to me how people can watch someone struggling to open a door, close a door, or pick up something, yet be totally blind to lending a hand. If you see that there is a human need or professional need, you stand out by responding to it.

Sally Jessy Raphael, the talk-show host and a former client, is a very caring and thoughtful person. She's a master of reaching out of her own comfort zone and doing for others. She was participating at an event, and just as I had put her in the car at the end — which is one of the things PR people do for their clients — she asked if she could give *me* a ride.

There are a lot of people tuning out the world around them. You can stand out and make an impact by not losing touch. Take some time to be friendly to the new kid in school. No matter where they came from, you can be sure they miss their buddies from their old school or their hometown. You may not become a best friend, but stepping outside the comfort zone to speak to the new kid can make a tremendous difference to both of you.

SAY "I'M SORRY"

Human beings try to put on a hard face. Kids try to be hard-core, to act like things don't bother them. But deep down, they hurt like everybody else. "I'm sorry" sounds weak; "I'm sorry" is not easy to say, especially when the action has resulted in injury or betrayal. Our egos get in the way. We might have to admit, "I was wrong."

That's usually when the hard shell comes up and we start to rationalize our actions. We can find all kinds of reasons why someone else is to blame or the circumstances were more than we could control.

Saying "I'm sorry" can mean breaking down some of the defenses we've put up to protect ourselves.

I'm Sorry and I Apologize

I'm sorry and I apologize
I'm sorry I apologize
I'm sorry and I realize
I'm sorry and I exercise my right to
Recognize I messed up and I'm sorry
My ego wants to find a way to make it not my fault
If I play the game just right I can blame you by default
I can make a list and itemize the things you've done to me
I can count them on my fingers, count 'em up like one two three
But the real deal is I'm sorry and I cannot justify that I've hurt you and then
Turn around and look you in the eye
If I go along and act like I didn't do a wrong
I'd be lying and defeat myself, lose the power to be strong
I would jeopardize our friendship and the good times that we had
And I'm hopin' if I apologize that you will not be mad and never be my

friend again and let us drift apart cuz you actually
are my best friend and it
would hurt me to my heart to know that you won't
talk to me or be there
when I'm down or smile when you see me and my
posse comin' roun'
I'm sorry and I apologize
I'm sorry I apologize
I'm sorry and I realize
I'm sorry and I exercise my right to
Recognize I messed up and I'm sorry
I messed up and I'm sorry
I messed up and I'm sorry
I messed up and I'm sorry

— Sharita Hunt

It is important to apologize when you do something wrong. It's a really, really hard thing to do but it builds you up in the eyes of other people when you are able to say, "I'm sorry," or are able to admit that you're wrong. It impresses the other person. It can also give them strength, and be an example of what to do and how to do it.

And when you receive the apology, keep in mind that to err is human, to forgive, divine. Say, "Apology accepted," and mean it!

Apology Accepted

Apology accepted that's all I've got to say
Even though you hurt my feelings in a deep and painful way
I admit that I would miss not to see you after class
or go and get a burger and lend you cash for gas
I would miss it not to help you with your biology
cuz I count you as my friend and I accept your apology
Yeah you made me angry, made me mad as a result
I respect that you admit it and can say it was your fault
I know it wasn't easy, it might take me quite a while
So let's just say it's done with, we are friends, we reconcile.
we are friends, we reconcile
we are friends, we reconcile
we are friends,
we reconcile.

— Sharita Hunt

ON THE DOWN-LOW

How to Apologize

Ms. Demeanor says:

- **Go to the person as soon as possible**
- **Don't rehash what was said, it will only hurt again.**
- **Be honest and sincere.**
- **Accept responsibility.**
- **Let the person know how much you value them and their friendship.**
- **Apologize — say you are sorry.**
- **Learn from the incident.**

Finally, make friends with yourself now. You'll have fewer regrets later. Treat yourself well. Eat healthy food, exercise, and get enough rest. Keep your grades up and don't be afraid to ask for help if you need it.

Surround yourself with people who are supportive and whom you can support and help. You don't need friends who put you down or laugh at your dreams.

Our world is moving fast and it's easy to get out of balance and spend a lot of time on one area of your life. Find time to slow down once in a while. Take time to think about where you're going and what you're doing. Don't be afraid to ask for help if you need it with schoolwork or life or work. Life is a blast when you realize it's not all about *me,* but *we.*

"No man is an island entire of itself; every man is a piece of the continent, a part of the main . . . Any man's death diminishes me, because I am involved in mankind . . ." — John Donne (1572–1631)

"It's not all about me. Helping someone else might make a real difference in his or her life. Such things as saying thank you and giving others moments of joy might also make their life much better. How you act can help them learn how to live their lives differently and be better people. Helping others is getting mine and that's the best way to get mine." — Mary

"What are you getting that you don't want others to have? Don't you think it is better if everyone gets something? Who are you, anyway, not to think about other people?" — Kim

8

IT'S THE "IN-CROWD" THAT MATTERS

"They set themselves apart from others — they are a clique. If your heart is set on getting into the "in" crowd and they say something about you, you can feel like you are marked for like, you know, "lights out." — Kareem

"People just invent that kind of thinking in their minds, you know, just to be cool. They see someone they think is better than they are, and they think they want to be in the "in" crowd. That kind of thinking comes from people who are just insecure and don't know who they are and where they are going." — Tiffany

We all need friends and folks to hang out with and have a good time. Most young people want to fit in, to be loved, and considered part of a crowd.

But the cost of fitting in can make you pay a price you never imagined! Choose your friends wisely. We tend to do the things our friends do.

I know you probably don't want to hear what it was like when I was growing up (a hundred years ago) but there's some benefit to paying attention to other people's experience.

In junior high school and high school I wanted to be like all the cool people. They were the ones who could stay out late for parties, whose parents didn't pick them up at midnight, who wore the most up-to-date clothes.

The cool people in junior high and high school got stuck in a routine and did not expose themselves to new and different things. As a result, they suffered in adulthood and became very, very, very limited.

The lives of "cool people" may look like a lot of fun right now. These people are the center of attention and are admired by a majority of the kids in your school. But someday these people will have to make it in the real world. When the competition is tough, it will take more than being cool to excel. So hang in there and don't be intimidated. I believe you'll do far better in life, in the long run, than many of the cool people. Just stay focused and on track.

If you are a nerd you have great things in store for you. Bill Gates, the richest man in America, was a nerd. Woodlyne Jean-Charles is a seventeen-year-old Chicago student who won a gold medal in the

NAACP Afro-Academic, Cultural, Technological and Scientific Olympics (ACT-SO) program. Woodlyne says, "I've been called nerd, geek, every name in the book. I really didn't let it faze me. I'm no nerd. I'm just a person who is very determined in life." *That's* cool!

ACCEPTING RIDICULE FOR DOING THE RIGHT THING

"You want to be popular and be with people who are popular, so sometimes it is hard to do the right thing and have friends at the same time. It's not always cool to do the right thing. People call you names sometimes and you can feel bad." — Jon

A lot of times the cool people make fun of the ones who are very serious about doing well in school. It doesn't make sense to be ridiculed for doing the right thing, but it happens. People who ridicule others need to feel better about themselves, so they put others down. It makes them feel superior.

It takes courage to do the right thing. Bullies

and kids with powerful personalities can be intimidating. They can make you feel foolish and call you names. Try to ignore them. Let their words roll off your back if you can. Remember you never, never, never, never lose when you do the right thing.

Now you may say, "But Terrie, what about the people who do the right thing and get screwed anyway?" Very good question. But you can't back away from the right thing just because it might not work out right now. That's where the courage part comes in. There's a saying, "If you don't stand for something you'll fall for anything." Stand for what is right no matter what the cool people say or do. People will respect you for having the courage to do the right thing — even if they never tell you.

STANDING OUT

"Sometimes people say things to you that make you feel bad because you stand out by having good grades. I find that I stand out in school and most people say things to me that would hurt some people. Some people who listen to what others say to them begin to slack off in their work." — Mary

Standing out is risky. You can stand out in a positive way or a negative way. I want to give you the tools to stand out and equip you for the long, fulfilling life I pray you'll have. But it's not easy; you have to be strong.

I've set up some pretty good rules that can lighten the load of establishing your place in the world. I think they will give you an edge in life and help you cope with setbacks.

Above all, it's never too early — or too late — to start standing out. No matter what your interests, good living and righteous thinking always stand out. When you think and live positively, it makes a difference in how you see the world. You'll think well of people rather than of ways to put them down. And it won't bother you if you're not just like everyone else.

Judith Jamison, artistic director of the Alvin Ailey Dance Theater, said once, "Learn the craft of knowing how to open your heart and to turn on your creativity. There's a light inside of you." You know the old church song, "This little light of mine, I'm gonna let it shine"? Let your light shine and you will stand out.

Next, get in the habit of excellence. Make sure your work is error-free. Mistakes in grammar or spelling will count against you in school — and when you start sending out résumés, those errors are a sure way to get your résumé, maybe even your career, tossed right into the old "circular file." And realize that good grades aren't enough. Astronomical SAT scores will help, but they're not guaranteed to get you into the college of your choice. You need to do your best in every area of your life.

Start now to stop, look, and listen to those who are worthy of your respect. Pay attention to a special event, birthday, or anniversary that comes up for someone you admire. Send that person a card. Find a way to develop a mentor relationship.

Meet new kids at school. Don't judge a person by outward appearances. Make an effort to delve into the person. What does she like to do for fun? What kinds of things does he read? What experiences has she lived through?

Don't sweat the people who try to put you down. When it's all said and done, twenty years from now you probably won't even remember their names.

MAKING FRIENDS WHO MATTER

The up-and-coming brother of a well-known black comedian lived in a fairly one-dimensional inner-city world. Trying to build his career, the brother started going out on the road, performing. He went across this country and around the world. Because of this adventure, the brother's whole world has opened up. Now one of his closest buddies is an Irish guy from Boston. Had he not stepped out of his comfort zone, he would never have found he had something in common with someone so different. It's important to expose yourself to different kinds of people because you will realize that we are much more alike than we are different.

If I had it to do all over again, I would have stepped a little more outside of my comfort zone. I would have made a conscious effort to do some things that were going to stretch my mind.

Stepping outside your comfort zone doesn't mean you need to be friends with everybody. It's wise to observe how a potential friend behaves. You don't have to be friends with everyone and you don't have to like everyone and not everyone is going to like you or want to be your friend. A lot of people you meet are potential friends, but your interests and temperaments can determine whether you become tight or not.

An important aspect of choosing your friends is knowing yourself. Understanding yourself — your values, likes, dislikes, goals, aspirations, and dreams. Otherwise, you could find yourself in a group of friends with whom you really don't have much in common. Or you could be with a group who could lead you away from your dreams. It's only natural that folks who hang out together influence one another.

There's an old saying, "Association brings about assimilation." Be careful that the friends you choose don't drain your physical, emotional, and spiritual resources. If they do, chances are you will become a physical, emotional, and spiritual drain on someone else. So look for friends who can build you up and support you and whose values and vibe you can support.

The cool people aren't the ones who matter. The people who matter are the ones with whom you can be your best self. I wouldn't trade places with any of the folks I wanted to be like a thousand years ago.

There will probably always be "in" crowds that will try to define what's cool. There will always be cliques and a group that will set themselves up as impenetrable. Be sure you know yourself. Because you are the one who matters.

"Just stop to think you are a unique individual. You are just as important as anyone is. The "in" crowd, the jocks, are perhaps so insecure and nervous they want you to be with them, but they don't think it is cool to let you know." — Joel

"I draw people to me. I have my own crew. Others now want to be in my group. It feels different now that I have a group of my own. Since I have been in my last year in high school, I have been considered a part of an "in" crowd. I do my own thing. I don't worry about other people and what they think. That's what I tell kids now: Just be yourself and if people don't like that, too bad. In the end you will be happier if you just stick to being who you are." — Darrell

"You should make the most of the time you have. Now is everything. No one is promised tomorrow or a rose garden even for today. You have to do the very best you know how and if now turns out to be everything, well, you will have no regrets." — Meghan

Okay, I'll admit it. I don't cook. But I know the difference between instant mashed potatoes and mashed potatoes from scratch. It takes longer to make mashed potatoes from scratch. They have to be peeled, boiled, mashed, buttered, milked, seasoned, and stirred. That's a lot of work, but they are so good. With instant you just add milk or water. That's it. They're okay — but they're nothing like the real thing. You may think this illustration is lame, but you and I both know time makes all the difference in life. There are just some things you have to wait for to see the successful result. Sometimes it's worth it to let "now" go in order to achieve something over the long run.

It's great to want to experience life here and

now — while you're young and can put your energy into pursuing all of your dreams. Don't forget, though, that what we do now has an effect on the future — immediate and distant.

Live in the now and plan for the future.

Live like there's no tomorrow and plan like you have forever.

Balance. Look for ways to balance between now and forever.

Anita Baker gave up a promising career after a number of very successful albums and winning several Grammys. She decided she wanted to live a quiet life with her husband, raising her children. Some might say that was the end of her career, but the reason most of us want to *have* a career and make money is to enjoy a life like hers.

My biggest decision was to establish myself professionally, and doing so meant that personal relationships and children were secondary. I looked up one day and realized a husband and kids really weren't to be. I decided early on to really invest my time and energy in a career, one that I wasn't trained for but I basically taught myself. That decision impacted my life forever and it's taken a while for me to learn how to have balance. Fortunately, I was able to experience parenthood by adopting Rocky, whom I met through a mentoring program, seven years ago. (And now, I'm looking for Mr. Right. Got any older friends?)

Decide what is important to you. What are the core values you can live by to guide your decisions? To live out these values, you'll need to use your time well.

What I've learned didn't come instantly and the lessons you learn will probably not be instant, either. The wisdom you gain will be the result of peeling, boiling, mashing, milking, and seasoning.

Our American culture can make "now" seem way more important than it is. Making money is important, but you don't have to make it all today. Being fulfilled in your relationships and life's work is more important — and those things always take time. Sex is great. But we are often pressured into sexual activity that's more about selfish satisfaction and manipulation. I'm not a prude, but don't let anybody tell you that you can't control yourself because you're young. That is a lie. Don't pay attention to those who try to make you do something — and tell you you're not cool if you don't.

* * *

So how do you know what to do "now" and what can wait until later? Angela Bassett, star of *How Stella Got Her Groove Back,* said, "When you're young, I think it's really important to follow that voice in your head that says, 'Just try it.' If it doesn't work out, at least you followed your dream. . . ."

Sound familiar? We've talked about paying close attention to that voice. You might be a little afraid of just going for it, but I say try. I would never have gone into the public relations field if I was scared to quit working at the hospital for the sake of security.

I have observed many people who have seized the day. Master P, recording artist and amazing entrepreneur, cannot be stopped. He is an artist who keeps branching out into all kinds of new areas. He is driven, and he goes for each new challenge that comes his way. In 1999, *Fortune* magazine described him as "a popular rapper, a sought-after actor, 6-foot 4-inch near NBA-caliber basketball player, a successful record and film producer, an enterprising fashion and toy entrepreneur ('Ya hear me?' the Master P doll roars), who founded perhaps the most scrutinized sports agency ever. He may also be the most intriguing executive in the music business."

According to *Fortune,* his net worth is $361 million. He grew up in the crime-infested Calliope projects in New Orleans. He was determined to get out and he did.

Master P did not stop at becoming successful. He brought along several of his friends and relatives, who now work with him in key positions in his corporation, No Limit.

Hot Boy (Jimmy Keller) is Master P's first cousin. Master P called him on the day he was released from prison after serving seven-and-a-half years for manslaughter. "He had left me a few messages, but I was too embarrassed to return his call," says Keller. "He finally got me, and he didn't say anything about where I'd been or what I'd done. He just came and got me and said, 'We got work to do.' He saved my life."

Master P knows the value of the here and now. Start now and don't stop reaching. Even if you are scared to death, go for your dreams. Start the race now!

GOING THE DISTANCE—PERSEVERANCE

Once you start, persistence is key. Persistence is the quality that separates those who make it from those who don't. Simply put: Those who make it, stay in the race. You can't win if you don't finish. Anyone can be persistent. Of course, quitting is easier. But if you truly want to make a difference you must challenge yourself constantly and never give up.

How do you stay in the race for a successful life? You *plan* to. You decide that you will. You set the goals and do the deeds — over time. But, bit by bit with patience, you keep at it.

For inspiration, I highly recommend *Chicken Soup for the Teenage Soul.* The Chicken Soup series offers stories to give you just that extra amount of insight and strength to stick with your objectives. Here is one story from the book:

Chris Samele's leg was severed through the knee in an automobile accident. Chris was on the basketball team, a talented athlete. As a result of the injury it looked as though he would not play again. You can guess where this story is going. Chris did play basketball. He had very painful and exhausting therapy and learned to use his prosthetic leg. After working very hard and playing basketball clumsily at first, he tried out for the junior varsity basketball team eleven months later and made it!

The Chicken Soup Editor's Note says, "Samele went on to star with the varsity basketball team at Torrington High School during his junior and senior years. Chris also played both singles and doubles on the school tennis team. He has played on the varsity tennis team at Western New England College in Springfield, Massachusetts, and has played intramural basketball at Western New England and in summer leagues in the Torrington area. Samele hopes to become a basketball coach."

Sometimes when I'm stuck or scared, I draw on the amazing things others are able to accomplish. It puts things in perspective.

Jennifer Lindsay, a nineteen-year-old violin virtuoso and 1999 *Essence* Magazine Award winner, suffered a loss of oxygen at birth that left her brain-damaged. Doctors predicted she would never develop normally. Jennifer's mother quit her job as a junior high school teacher to devote all her time to working intensively with her daughter. The result of her perseverance was that at age three Jennifer was reading at a second-grade level. At five, she was playing the violin. At thirteen, she started taking college courses and at sixteen scored 1560 out of 1600 on her SAT. But just imagine if her mother had not put in the time during those early years, taking her daughter to doctors and childhood development experts and teaching Jennifer at home. But it doesn't stop there. Jennifer gives back. She tutors, gives musical performances at rest homes, churches, and private organizations, and maintains a 4.0 grade-point average.

Jennifer Lindsay is a product of her mother's perseverance — and her own.

When you stick with something, it's not only for yourself — you may also inspire others to persevere.

Charlie Ward was recognized as being one of the greatest college athletes in the world, yet people said he was too short, he was a Christian, didn't have any "bad-boy" flair, and he would never make it in the NBA. He wasn't drafted in a high enough round in the NFL — even though he won the Heisman Trophy. Fortunately, he was drafted by the New York Knicks with a wonderful contract. He was offered an incredible salary. In the first year or two, critics still questioned his height, his ability, his game. In the 2000 playoffs, in front of the very people who criticized him, he saved two games and allowed the Knicks to advance to the finals.

There was a time when Eddie Murphy was getting a lot of unfair and somewhat negative press for making films that weren't breaking $100 million. Some said he was washed up. He came to have the attitude that "if that's the way to be washed up, then shower me any day!" because all his films more than recouped the initial investment. They always broke some kind of record. And he was pulling in more money than Tom Cruise. Even the biggest celebs have to persevere in the face of negativity and press on for an even brighter future.

The problem with now versus forever is that we can only see the now. Going the distance, persevering, means we have to believe that sacrificing something today will make something worthwhile in the future.

"When I was young, I was perpetually overconfident or insecure. Either I felt completely useless, unattractive, and worthless, or that I was pretty much a success and everything I did was bound to succeed.

"When I was confident, I could overcome the hardest challenges but all it took was a small setback for me to be sure that I was utterly worthless . . . self-confidence had nothing to do with success.

"Every goal I set, every recognition I craved, made anything I actually did seem paltry by comparison. And whether I experienced it as a failure or a triumph was utterly dependent on my mood."
— *The Reader* by Bernhard Schlink

Does everyone feel that way? I think so. There are times when it doesn't matter how much positive feedback you get — you still feel as though everything is totally out of control. There are days when you feel you simply can't do anything right. Why did you bother, anyway? And don't let somebody look at you funny. Forget it. You're reduced to tears or feel ready to take it outside.

And your parents and other adults have the nerve to tell you it's just a phase.

Feelings don't have to justify or determine your actions. You have to get on with it regardless of how you feel. Do not deny what you feel or decide that what you feel is not important. Instead, decide that as important as your feelings are, they cannot determine how you react to every situation.

Check out the situation. Try to take time to think it through as logically as possible. If you're upset, remove yourself from the scene for a while before you say or do anything. Even if it looks like you can't just walk away, remember what is *true* about you — not what others think or say to provoke you. Otherwise you'll become a volatile powder keg just waiting for someone to strike the match so you can explode — or develop an ulcer.

We've talked about this before, but it bears repeating that this is one of the reasons you have parents, friends, and counselors at school. Don't try to go through stuff alone. Trust me, there is someone who can relate to what you're going through because they've already been there, done that, and come out on the other side a little older and wiser.

Mason Betha, a.k.a. Mase, overcame the challenge of life in the inner city through music. He worked with and wrote for Sean "Puffy" Combs. Though he describes himself as having been a loner for a long time, it didn't keep him from working with Puff Daddy and the late Notorious B.I.G.

Mase's slow rapping style was ridiculed at first but regardless of how he felt about the criticism, he continued. In a *Newsweek* article Mase says, "I rap slow, and people made fun of it, but now you hear more and more rappers slowing down . . . I made that happen." At the age of twenty, Mase has given up the rap scene because he wants to do more. "It's time for me to serve God in His way. I've always known that there was something else out there for me to do. Not just this stuff because, like I said before, this isn't real and I gotta deal with reality. There's no other way to stay true to the game — the real game of life." What are his plans? Go back to school and get a degree in psychology and work with kids. He's on a mission. Every mission is a challenge, but if the goals are clear for you, your momentary feelings won't be too fierce a challenge.

GIVING IS THE GREATEST FEELING

One way to get out of yourself and your feelings is to give to someone else.

Volunteering is a way to get involved in your community and give back. Look in the Yellow Pages under Social Service Organizations and you will find lots of organizations that could use your youth and your enthusiasm.

During the holiday season leading to Thanksgiving, Chanukah, Christmas, and Kwaanza, there are all kinds of appeals for the public to reach out to the poor. Most of the appeals are for monetary contributions. Now you will not always have money to give. But you do have time and yourself, which are just as valuable — if not more so.

Nickelodeon's Big Help is a huge event that encourages kids to volunteer in their neighborhood doing everything from fund-raising to helping kids with cancer to cleaning up parks in their communities. Since Nickelodeon started Big Help, thousands of kids have donated millions of hours to their communities. Its Web site has letters from kids who share their experiences and how much they enjoyed helping their community. One story in particular is very touching. Brendan Meyer, sixteen, was asked to help an autistic young man of the same age to learn a dance routine for a variety show. Brendan wrote, "Kevin and I spent many hours in that theater, but it all seemed to pay off come opening night. Just the feeling I got seeing Kevin's eyes light up seemed to be a great reward. Just knowing that I could help somebody that much feels like a blessing."

REAL STORIES

I Just Feel That Way

They called themselves "Dee-vaz" because they felt like they were extreme. Bigger than life. They lived by the creed, "How I feel is who I am."

Stephanie, Cassandra (Cass for short), and Genna had been friends ever since they mounted their own production of *For Colored Girls Who Have Considered Suicide When the Rainbow is Enuf* by Ntozake Shange. The drama teacher was almost clueless since he wasn't black, but Stephanie's mom had an actress friend who was able to tell them what was really going on. Though it was kinda shocking to some people, overall their play was well received.

Now they had decided that they were rappers. Stephanie had written one so-so good rhyme. But as they all sat around one day talking about how they just feel the way they do, a rap started to be born. When they finished, they decided they would compete in the senior class talent competition. They were sure that lots of kids did things just because they felt like it. Most of the time it didn't mean anything except that's how they felt now. Genna really wanted the kids in school to know that they were not alone in anything they felt.

Stephanie's response was, "Gaaawwwd, do we have to be relevant? Can't we just do the rap and have a good time?"

Genna's mom said she hoped the rap would help someone. Her favorite phrase was "you never know who is gonna get something good from what you do." She even helped them with their costumes. They got Stephanie's brother to lay down a rhythm track for them and Genna's folks let them practice in their basement.

By the night of the competition they were ready. Stephanie wore her favorite leopard pants. Cass wore a short skirt with a shawl and platform shoes, and Genna wore pajamas like Ally McBeal's.

The stage manager called "places." They got into position behind the curtain and whispered "break a leg" to one another as the curtain open. The spotlight hit them and the rhythm began.

Stephanie
I wanna put me on some cheetah-patterned pants, a halter made of leather and lots of rings of gold. I'm gonna pull my hair up into a spray and tie it with a scrunchie made of gold lamé. I'm gonna do what I can to create lots of drama and be just like a hoochie mama. And stay just like that all day, I don't care, 'cause I feel that way.

Cass
Gonna wiggle my booty up and down the street and wear six-inch platforms on my size-eight feet and if anybody has anything to say, I don't care, 'cause I feel that way. I don't care, 'cause I feel that way. I might wear me skirt way down below my knees, and white tennis shoes if you please, ain't gonna wear no makeup no makeup at all and be plain as can be just like baby doll. Then maybe later on, on that same day, I'll go back to hoochie mama and know what I'ma say, I'm hoochie mama now, 'cause I feel that way!

Genna
I'ma paint my toes a fluorescent green, wear a scowl on my face and look very mean then bust out laffing for no real good reason 'cept to be say to my posse, "I'm only teasin'." If they catch an attitude and treat me rude I won't be nasty, crude, or lewd, I'll turn my head and just walk away 'cause I don't care, I just feel that way.

Stephanie
Gonna make my eyes look slanty and cool, I'm even gonna be an hour early to school. That'll blow their minds when they come that day, but I don't care, I just feel that way. I'm gonna pay attention in geometry, then I'ma take the test and get better than a B and then I'm gonna plan my higher education (I think I'll ask my dad to define miscegenation) and when he starts to think "She's lost her mind an' gone astray," I'll turn my head and walk away, I don't care, I just feel that way.

Cass
When I lower my head to dream the night away and think about the things that I said that day, the way

I played and studied and all I can hold my head up and really walk tall and even with the drama in cheetah-patterned tights and home from the mall before ten o'clock nights, I'm not ashamed of anything I did and what I had to say, 'cause the real truth is, I just feel that way.

Genna
And every time I start to feel weird
    Funny or alone,
    I go to my mom
    Or pick up the phone
    Call me up somebody that I know will care

Stephanie
Call me up somebody that I know will be there.

Cass
Who's gonna wanna listen to what I've got to say

Stephanie, Cass, Genna
'Cause that's what friends do when you feel that way.
That's what friends do when you feel that way.
That's what friends do when you feel that way.

They hit their final pose, the lights went black and the crowd erupted. The girls danced off and the next act was announced.

After the whole thing was over, their moms were waiting for them with big hugs and high fives. They were good and they knew it. The feeling wasn't just something vague and undefinable. They had done something they were very proud of that was not just a feeling, it was real and tangible. The Dee-Vaz had inspired the crowd. Everyone had applauded. And it felt good.

There is more to the movement of the universe than feelings. And no one has to be or feel all alone. No matter how you feel there are people who care about you, people who can be there for you, to keep you from doing something really stupid or who will encourage you to do something truly cool.

FACTS ARE FRIENDS

Mark Jenkins is a trainer to the stars and he works with Mary J. Blige, D'Angelo, Johnnie Cochran, Busta Rhymes, and Dr. Ruth. He told me about a situation with an employee who was on the road with D'Angelo. The employee had become upset because he didn't feel he was being paid as much as someone on staff with more experience. He decided to handle the situation in a very immature fashion and did not call Mark while he was on the road for thirty days. When he got back he didn't call for another three days. I asked Mark how was it possible to not flip out completely. He said that through a lot of reading and meditation he had learned to detach himself from his feelings about the situation.

I know this is hard, but don't let your feelings be the main guiding force in your life. Your feelings can be fragile and they can fool you. They can cause you to misunderstand a situation or make an irrational decision.

Often, you have to pay more attention to the facts than to what you feel. For instance, your girlfriend breaks off the relationship. All right, nobody likes being dumped. It hurts your feelings. It makes you feel just plain ol' bad. You could find yourself doing some real harm. What's real? What are the facts? There are plenty of people in the world who are looking to love and be loved. There are plenty of people who actually get over being dumped and later meet the person who is, in fact, their soul mate.

You feel like a teacher doesn't like you. If you know for a fact that you have done nothing to the teacher, then you have to rely on the facts and do your best. That's all you are responsible for. The fact is there are going to be people who will not like you for all kinds of crazy reasons that have little or nothing to do with you. Then they'll try to make you feel bad by dissing you or not speaking to you or doing something ridiculous. They may not like your manner or the way you speak. That's when you have to rely on the facts. The fact is you are valuable, special, worthy. These facts are your friends.

I'm not saying deny your feelings. I'm just saying don't allow them to be so important that you make silly mistakes because you didn't take the time to evaluate the facts.

And, yes, there are times when your gut response or feeling is right. The hard part is discerning the difference between your feelings and facts. Talk with an objective friend, parent, or counselor who can help you sort out the differences. The feelings you have may be so wrong you wonder if you've lost your mind. On the other hand, you could be absolutely and totally on the money.

When we started the journey through this book, one of the first things we recognized is that life is not fair. That everything is not cut-and-dried. There are issues of right and wrong and there are gray areas that are not so clear-cut. That's life. But my prayer for you is simple: that as you grapple with the difficult issues of life you will respond to those feelings that propel you to want to be significant in this world — look for the facts and the people who will help you do just that.

Create a good life for yourself.
Terrie

AFTER-WORD

One who gains strength by overcoming obstacles possesses the only strength which can overcome adversity.
— Albert Schweitzer,
Physician, missionary,
philosopher Nobel Laureate

Congratulations on finishing the book! I had a good time writing this book for you — our leaders of tomorrow — and I hope that you gain some inspiration from my experiences.

Our daily interactions and experiences lead to learning. My aim was to provide you with the motivation and support to stay strong and persevere as you strive for the goals you have set for yourself. What else would I like to see happen? For you to reexamine, challenge, and push yourself further than you ever thought possible.

So let me know if it worked. I'd love to hear from you. Write me at Columbus Circle Station/P.O. Box 20227, New York, NY 10023. As I mentioned in my first book, *The Personal Touch,* I make a point to read all letters and try to respond. With your help, in passing this message on, we can continue to do God's work. As always, *Stay Strong.*

Love,
Terrie Williams

SELECTED BIBLIOGRAPHY

This is not a comprehensive list of every source I've mentioned in the book — instead it's simply a list of the books I relied on.

Canfield, Jack, Mark Victor Hansen and Kimberly Kirberger, eds. *Chicken Soup for the Teenage Soul: 101 Stories of Live, Love and Learning.* Deerfield Beach: Health Communications, Inc., 1997.

Delany, Sarah and A. Elizabeth. *Having Our Say: The Delany Sisters' First 100 Years.* Kodansha America, Inc., 1993.

Manheim, Camryn. *Wake Up, I'm Fat!* New York: Broadway Books, 1999.

Mariotti, Steve. *The Young Entrepreneur's Guide to Starting and Running a Business.* New York: Crown Publishing Group, 1999.

Mitchell, Mary. *Dear Ms. Demeanor: The Young Person's Etiquette Guide to Handling Any Social Situation with Confidence and Grace.* Chicago: NTC/Contemporary Publishing, 1995.

Reisfeld, Randi and Marie T. Morreale. *Got Issues Much? Celebrities Share Their Traumas and Triumphs.* New York: Scholastic, Inc., 1999.

Souljah, Sister. *The Coldest Winter Ever.* New York, Pocket Books, 1999.

Underhill, Daryl Ott, compiler. *Every Woman Has A Story: Many Voices, Many Lessons, Many Lives.* New York, Warner Books, 1999.

Williams, Terrie. *The Personal Touch: What You Really Need to Succeed in Today's Fast-paced Business World.* New York: Warner Books, 1994.

Zimmerman, William. *Book of Questions to Keep Thoughts and Feelings.* New York: Guarionex Press, Limited, 1990.

RECOMMENDED READING

Canfield, Jack, Irene Dunlap, Patty Hansen, and Mark Victor Hansen, eds. *Chicken Soup for the Kid's Soul: 101 Stories of Courage, Hope and Laughter.* Deerfield Beach: Health Communications, 1998.

DeJesus, Edward. *The Young Adult's Guide to "Making It": Successful Strategies for Getting and Keeping a Job.* Gaithersburg: Youth Development & Research Fund, 1997.

Forsyth, Sondra. *Girls Seen and Heard: 52 Lessons For Our Daughters.* New York: The Putnam Publishing Group, 1998.

Freeman, Lucille Usher and Janet Chatham Bell, eds. *Stretch Your Wings: Famous Black Quotations for Teens.* New York: Little, Brown & Company, 1999.

Post, Elizabeth L., and Joan M. Coles. *Emily Post's Teen Etiquette.* New York: HarperCollins, 1995.

Zimmerman, Bill. *A Book of Sunshine: Featuring Tiny Miracles, Moving Clouds and Sunbursts.* Naperville: Sourcebooks, 1997.

Zimmerman, Bill. *Idea Catcher for Kids.* Cincinnati: Writers Digest Books, 2000.

Zimmerman, Bill. *Little Book of Joy: An Interactive Journal For Thoughts, Prayers, and Wishes.* Center City: Hazelden Information Education, 1995.

ACKNOWLEDGMENTS

Love, Appreciation, and Thanks to:

Mom, for the 24/7 unwavering support and for nurturing a generation of kids who will be better because of your love and guidance.

Dad, for your gentle spirit and for showing me by example how to make room in the house for those less fortunate.

Lani, for being a loving sister and for making me laugh. And my brother-in-law, for loving Lani and me so strong.

Rocky, my son and my friend, for lighting up my universe with your heart, your spirit, and wisdom.

Joe Cooney, master wordsmith, for your wise counsel and guidance on this project and for saving my butt over the years — over & over.

Tony Wafford, for teaching me powerful life lessons and that no matter what happens in life, Stay Strong! (I took that from you many years ago and made it *my* signature.) P.S. Who's Quick?

"Queen" Jae Je Simmons, my sistah friend, for reminding me there was a "Personal Touch" for teens and for guiding me there with love and wisdom — and salve.

Rachel Noerdlinger, my "daughter" — the new PR diva, for your love and support and feedback on this project — and to my future teen Khari who always brings a smile to my face.

Xavier Artis, for hearing me when I don't want you to and listening when I don't think you are.

For my Scholastic family — Judy Newman and Maggie Kneip, for appreciating the vision of life lessons for teens and for lighting the fire.

Jean Feiwel, for the Scholastic stamp of approval and for your infinite wisdom in asking Adrenne Ingrum to anchor the ship.

Kate Egan, for being the "411" lifeline always with a smile and the right information — and most of all for seeing that *Stay Strong* as the book's title was right in front of our faces (on the voice mail, the note cards, etc. . . .).

Elizabeth Parisi and McDavid Henderson, for the brilliant artistic interpretation of *Stay Strong*.

Jennifer Pasanen, Steven Kasdin, Kris Moran, Charisse Meloto, for your care, attention, and great marketing ideas.

Adrienne Ingrum, whose vision, light, patience, gentle spirit, and editorial genius guided this voyage. You are the best! You delivered!

Sharita Hunt, for your amazingly creative gifts, ways, and words — and for going above and beyond.

Eleanor Henderson, for loving kids and getting the right stuff from them.

Tanya McKinnon, my agent, for being the brilliant, loving, and guiding genius that you are. I'd walk through fire for you, too.

Tanya Odums, for organizing the Kaplan House guys to participate and share their life lessons — and for giving your all to them.

All my guys at Kaplan, for giving of yourselves and your time for this project: Willy N. Pino, James Davis, Danny Hernandez, Miguel Rodriguez, David Burstine, Jahmod White, Fernando Dessett, Rafael Marcano, Urcania Castillo, Aisha Odums, Nurse Lewis.

The Horace Mann High School students from the Bronx, for contributing your words of wisdom.

The TWA family: Tola Ozim, Nbiyeas Mullins, Michelle Robinson, Jennifer Solar, Natiki Montana, Crystal Robinson, Jacqueline Dolly, Regina Phillips.

Queen Latifah, for graciously giving your time and words of wisdom. In all endeavors you reach out with your heart, spirit, and mind.

Rita Owens — another beautifully spirited

woman. Your interest in the well-being of our youth is extraordinary; thanks for having Latifah!

Teens who have a special place in my heart and are going places in this world. Look out for them! Daniel Miller, Diamond Miller, Courtnei Evans, Bria Murphy, Jourdan Francis, Juan Rosas, Khalid Sumner, Hanif Sumner, Johnnie Williams III, Kate Carcaterra, Nick Carcaterra, Darren Harris, Hydeia Broadbent, Jovon Hoskins, James Grimes, Elias Kelley, Randy Croudy, Terry Ann Williams, Sharelle Conde, Cara Reaves.

Friends who endorsed *Stay Strong*: Chris Rock, Shaquille O'Neal, Sean Combs, Johnnie L. Cochran, Charlie Ward, Tavis Smiley, Montel Williams, E. Lynn Harris, Tyra Banks, Judge Greg Mathis, Charlotte Brandon, Shirley Garnett, Russell Simmons, Chris Cuomo, Ananda Lewis, Marian Wright Edelman.

For my family: Aunt Joe, Uncle Floyd, Aunt T, Aunt Bea, Aunt Louise, Pat, Gene, Alex, Twanna, Wesley, Nathan, Bernice, Valerie & James, Tony.

Other friends who supported me in this project in word, thought, or deed: Becky Gatling, Lucille Harrison, Malaak Compton-Rock, Donnie Wilson, Lisa Crapps, Estilita Ward, Ed Lewis, Khephra Burns, Doug Brown, Vernon Slaughter. Alan Gansberg, Leon Carter, Carol Salter, Ray Gerald, Maureen Malone, Chris Dudley, Latifa Whitlock, Mark Jones, Susan Toepfer, Helen Goss, Rita Ewing, Mac De La Cruz, Sir Shadow, Shellie Anderson, Joann Davis, Iyanla Vanzant, Adeyemi Bandele, Marvet Britto, Arthel Neville, Sharon Krassney, Peter Campbell, Lisa Clayton Robinson, Judy Rosemarin.

Those special souls "on special assignment" who understand there are no other people's children: Ayala Donchin, Stephanie Dyer, Walter McCarty, Richie Parker, George Daniels, Chris Cathcart, Richard Green, Joline Godfrey, Derek Speight, Steve Marriotti, Sheryl Miller, Al Morgan, Marva Smalls, Leon Carter, Rosie O'Donnell, Charlie & Tonja Ward, Marilyn Artis, Robin Kearse, Maurice DuBois, John Bess, Brenda Blackmon, Mary Grace Eapen, Debby Peppers, Zeke Mowatt, George Kilpatrick, Hans & Ivan Hageman, George Andros, Ken Knuckles, Joe Brooks, Mark Breland, Jackie Joyner-Kersee, Colin Powell, Bill Cosby, Oprah Winfrey, Ed DeJesus, Lou Gelormino, Marc Pollick, Lisa Davis, Lori S. Grey, Lisa Erika James, Lenora Fulani, Cheryl Rozier.

O.M.T. (One More Thing): Thanks to the following organizations for bringing out the kid in all of us: Scholastic; *Nickelodeon; Channel One; BET Teen Summit; MTV; Teen People; Kidpreneurs; YWCA; YMCA; Girl Scouts; Boy Scouts; Voices of the Children; The Valley, Inc.; Chicken Soup for the Teenage Soul;* Yellow Ribbon Suicide Prevention Program; *People Magazine* & The Digital Heroes Campaign; Giving Back Fund; VOICES of the Children, Children's Defense Fund, Public Allies New York, Shaka Franklin Foundation for Youth.

In loving memory of Aunt Helen, chairman of the board; Dontae Skinner, Christine Doles, Michael Emme; and Reggie Harris; and Vickie Klein, my kindergarten teacher.

She's a social worker by training. She's a public relations professional by design. She's an author, a lecturer, a deal maker, and an activist.

Terrie opened The Terrie Williams Agency in 1988 with superstar Eddie Murphy and jazz legend Miles Davis as her first clients. Today, the agency is considered one of the country's premiere firms specializing in public relations, corporate affairs, community relations, marketing, corporate diversity, and special events management.

Terrie Williams is also the author of the best-selling business book *The Personal Touch: What You Really Need to Succeed in Today's Fast-paced Business World*, which includes a foreword by comedian Bill Cosby.